Seafood Favorites

Seafood
Favorites

**Recipes from
authors and staff of
International Marine
Publishing Company**

Camden, Maine

Typeset by The Key Word, Inc., Belchertown, Massachusetts
Printed and bound by BookCrafters, Inc., Chelsea, Michigan
Designed by Amy Fischer
Cover illustration by Jeanne P. Fullilove

Published by International Marine Publishing Company
21 Elm Street, Camden, Maine 04843
(207) 236-4342

Contents

Publisher's Preface

Ideas for books take shape in many ways. Sometimes a light bulb goes off in a single brilliant mind, and lo! – there is a full-blown concept for a good book. Other times a group of editors may brainstorm their way to a plan for a good book. The idea for this good book, on the other hand, began to take shape slowly in the hallways and offices at International Marine with a throw-away comment here and a tongue-in-cheek remark there.

At some point the thing must have reached a critical mass—probably on one of those days when the most fastidious of our staff lunch-eaters were once again driven from the galley area by one particular staffer bringing in still more pungent fish chowder—for, without any of us realizing what had happened, we were faced with a book idea with a life of its own: Let's ask all our authors to send in their favorite seafood recipes with suitable yarns for seasoning.

Somebody said, "Why leave out the staff?" Why indeed?

So the call went out, and the seafood recipes began pouring in from the four corners of the United States, from far-flung islands, and even from roast-beefy old England. And some had the local postmark of Camden, Maine.

Some of the recipes were original; others were borrowed from friends and relatives. (I wondered about the propriety of this borrowing business until I sat down to prepare my own contribution and realized the obvious thing to do was share a few recipes of one of the great seafood cooks of the world, maybe the best in the whole South County of Rhode Island, my father-in-law, Lewis R. Greene.) All make guaranteed good eating.

Anyway, here you have it, our seafood favorites. Chow down in good health!

Roger C. Taylor
International Marine

List of Contributors

Authors Etc.

Howard Barnes
  The Backyard Boatyard
Bill Belcher
  Wind-Vane Self-Steering: How to Plan and Make Your Own
Fred P. Bingham
  Practical Yacht Joinery: Tools, Techniques, Tips
Eva Palasti Brown
  The Blue Water Cook Book
Mike Brown
  The Maine Lobster Book
  Saturday Cove
Jim Brown
  The Case for the Cruising Trimaran
Brainerd Chapman
  *Dream Cruise: From the Fjords of Norway to the Caribbean
    Islands*
Michael Martin Cohen, M.D.
  Dr. Cohen's Healthy Sailor Book
Roger Duncan
  Eastward
  Friendship Sloops
G.D. Dunlap
  Navigating and Finding Fish with Electronics
  Successful Celestial Navigation with H.O. 229

Patrick and June Ellam
Wind Song: Our Ten Years in the Yacht Delivery Business

Brian Fagan
Bareboating around the World

Mrs. Weston Farmer
From My Old Boat Shop (by Weston Farmer)

Craig Gilborn, Curator of The Adirondack Museum
The Adirondack Guide-Boat (by Kenneth and Helen Durant)

Jay S. Hanna
Marine Carving Handbook

Richard Henderson
Choice Yacht Designs
East to the Azores: A Guide to Offshore Passage-Making
John G. Alden and His Yacht Designs
Philip L. Rhodes and His Yacht Designs
The Racing-Cruiser, Second Edition
Sea Sense, Second Edition
Singlehanded Sailing: The Experiences and Techniques of the Lone Voyagers

Carl D. Lane
Go South Inside: Cruising the Inland Waterway

John Lewis
Restoring Vintage Boats

Paul Lipke
Plank on Frame: The Who, What and Where of 150 Boatbuilders

Richard M. Mitchell
The Steam Launch

Frank Mulville
Single-Handed Cruising and Sailing

Lesley Newhart
Bareboating around the World (photographer)

Ross Norgrove
Blueprint for Paradise: How to Live on a Tropic Island
The Charter Game: How to Make Money Sailing Your Own Boat
The Cruising Life
Cruising Rigs and Rigging

Warren Norville
Celestial Navigation Step by Step, Second Edition
Coastal Navigation Step by Step

Harold H. Payson
Instant Boats

Phil Schwind
Cape Cod Fisherman
Clam Shack Cookery
Making a Living Alongshore
Practical Shellfish Farming

Walter J. Simmons
Lapstrake Boatbuilding
Lapstrake Boatbuilding, Volume 2

Edward W. Smith, Jr.
Workaday Schooners

Jerry Stelmok
Building the Maine Guide Canoe

Eleanor Stephens
Traditions and Memories of American Yachting Complete Edition
(by W.P. Stephens)

Robert M. Steward
Boatbuilding Manual, Second Edition

Roger C. Taylor
The Elements of Seamanship
Good Boats
More Good Boats
Still More Good Boats
The Fourth Book of Good Boats

Chris Thompson
The Care and Repair of Small Marine Diesels

Allan H. Vaitses
Boatbuilding One-Off in Fiberglass
Covering Wooden Boats with Fiberglass
Lofting

Mark White
Building the St. Pierre Dory

International Marine Staff

Kathleen Brandes
Jane Brooks
Wanda Clossey
Jonathan Eaton
Pat Feener
April Jenkins
Nan Kulikauskas
Linda Massey
Ardie Millay
Kathleen Pieri
Lori Renn
Roger C. Taylor
Dot Williams

appetizers

Shrimp *Catticus Rex*

Catticus Rex visited many ports in Spain and Portugal, where prawns and shrimp are abundant. We love garlic, so we concocted a sinfully powerful appetizer for unsuspecting guests.

Serves 4–6 thirsty people

4–6 tablespoons olive or other vegetable oil
6 garlic cloves minced (more if you wish)
1 pound shelled shrimp or prawns, cooked or uncooked (The large prawns
    found in places like Mexico are ideal.)
a pinch of salt
pepper to taste
a substantial pinch of oregano
parsley

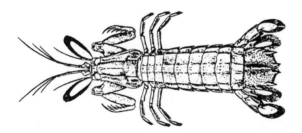

Heat the oil in a small frying pan over moderate-low heat. Add the garlic and shake it around until the oil is noticeably flavored. Add the shrimp, salt, pepper, and oregano. Cook slowly until the shrimp are well flavored, but still tender. Transfer the contents of the pan, juice and all, onto a suitable platter, garnish with parsley, and serve while still hot. The shellfish can be eaten as is, pronged on cocktail sticks, or served on stoned wheat crackers with sour cream.

Brian Fagan

CLAM PUFFS

Makes about 36 puffs

4 ounces cream cheese	1 tablespoon grated onion
1½ cups minced clams	1 beaten egg white
1 teaspoon Worcestershire sauce	crackers or toast triangles

Beat the cream cheese until smooth. Blend in the clams, Worcestershire sauce, and onion. Fold in the egg white. Pile the mixture on crackers or toast and bake at 450 degrees for about 3 minutes or until lightly browned.

Eleanor Stephens
(daughter of W.P. Stephens)

HOT CLAM DIP

8 ounces cream cheese
1 can or 1 cup minced clams
1 garlic clove, crushed

1 teaspoon Worcestershire sauce
potato chips

Place the cream cheese in a double boiler and stir with a whisk until softened. Stir in the minced clams, Worcestershire sauce, garlic juice (or ½ teaspoon garlic powder). Blend well. Serve hot with potato chips.

Eleanor Stephens
(daughter of W.P. Stephens)

CLAM SPREAD

Great for a good-sized party!

6 cans minced clams
3 packages cream cheese
crackers

Mush the cream cheese and clams together, cover, and refrigerate for about 1 hour. Spread on crackers with a knife.

Dot Williams

GREEK FISHERMAN'S HORS D'OEUVRE

I really don't want to share my famous recipes with others, but there is one exception because it is too good to keep. It is an exciting, salty-type thing that boat people should love.

For each serving:

1 saltine
a little butter
1 ¼-inch hard-boiled egg slice per cracker
1 sardine per cracker

The basic ingredient here is a saltine. As received from the manufacturer, it is raw, so to speak. Lightly spread the saltine with butter and broil in a toaster oven until golden brown. When cool, this is now known as a Georgia cracker. On top of the cracker place a slice of hard-boiled egg. The ¼-inch thickness is slightly greater than that produced by one of those wire-type egg slicers, but the difference is worthwhile. Select a slice with the maximum amount of yolk. The cracker-and-egg assembly is then topped off with a sardine. Wash down with red wine, 1 large glass.

Note: Do not prepare more of these hors d'oeuvres than can be used at one time, because they do not store well.

Robert M. Steward

Crabmeat Canapés

Makes 48

1 stick butter, softened	½ teaspoon garlic salt
1 jar Old English cheese	6–7 ounces crabmeat, canned
1½ teaspoons mayonnaise	or fresh
	6 English muffins, split

Mix the first 5 ingredients and spread on muffin halves. Cut each half into 4 pie-shaped pieces. Freeze the canapés on a cookie sheet, then store in freezer bag. Broil before serving.

Howard Barnes

Hot Crab Dip

We go to our friends' home every year at Christmas time for a cocktail party, and this dip is a big hit with everyone.

8 ounces cream cheese	½ teaspoon salt
1 teaspoon milk	½ teaspoon pepper
6½ ounces crabmeat	⅓ cup slivered almonds
1 teaspoon onion juice	paprika
½ teaspoon horseradish	

Blend the cream cheese and milk. Add the crabmeat, onion juice, horseradish, salt, and pepper. Place in an ovenproof dish, sprinkle with almonds and paprika, and bake at 375 degrees for 15 minutes.

Richard M. Mitchell

SEVICHE

Serves 6 as a first course, considerably more as hors d'oeuvres

1½ pounds raw scallops
½ cup fresh lime juice
½ cup fresh lemon juice
½ cup olive oil
¼ cup chopped scallions
¼ cup parsley, finely chopped

1 garlic clove, minced
1½ teaspoons salt
1 teaspoon cracked black pepper
4–6 drops Tabasco sauce
fresh coriander, chopped

Quarter the scallops if they are large sea scallops, and leave them whole if they are small bay scallops. Place the scallops in an enamel or pottery bowl and cover with lime and lemon juices. Cover the bowl and marinate in the refrigerator 4–6 hours. The marinade will "cook" the scallops. Drain. Mix the olive oil, scallions, parsley, garlic, salt, pepper, and Tabasco sauce. Pour over the scallops and toss gently. Chill for at least half an hour. Sprinkle with the coriander, arrange attractively on lettuce leaves or spear with toothpicks, and serve.

Kathleen Brandes

GEFILTE FISH

Serves 8–10

2 pounds carp, pike, whitefish,
  or a combination
1 large onion, sliced (save the skin)
1 large carrot, sliced
2¼ cups water

a dash of salt and pepper
2 eggs
2–3 tablespoons fine cracker crumbs
salt and pepper
horseradish

Fillet the fish (save the skin and bones) and set aside. Place the onion, its skin, and the carrot in a large pot. Add 2 cups of the water, salt and pepper, and the bones and skin of the filleted fish. Bring to a boil.

Put the fish fillets through a food processor or grinder. Add the eggs, cracker crumbs, salt, pepper, and the remaining ¼ cup water to the ground fish. Mix well and form into small football-shaped patties.

Gently lower these into the broth. Simmer slowly, covered, for 1 hour. Take the lid off the pot and simmer for another half hour, adding water as necessary. Allow to cool, then refrigerate. Remove the patties from the jelly. Serve chilled with horseradish.

Michael Martin Cohen, M.D.

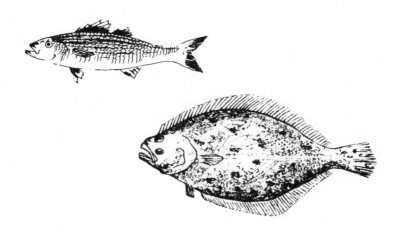

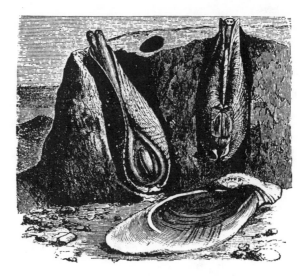

GUNKHOLE DELIGHT

For each serving:

a cracker
a "slick" of peanut butter
a bit of cold fish
a gob of horseradish

You take any kind of cracker (Ritz, soda, toastie, etc.) and place on it a slick of peanut butter. Then you mush over that a bit of cold fish, shrimp, or crabmeat, even a sardine, and over that a gob of horseradish. Be sure to warn your guests: Fresh horseradish can sting!

Carl D. Lane

Dr. Cohen's Cold Salmon Loaf

Makes 1 loaf

1 pound pink or red salmon
8 ounces cream cheese, softened
1 teaspoon white horseradish
¼ teaspoon salt
1 tablespoon lemon juice

2 teaspoons chopped onion
¼ teaspoon liquid smoke
½ cup pecans
3 tablespoons chopped parsley

Mix all the ingredients except the pecans and parsley. Shape into a loaf and roll in a mixture of the pecans and parsley. Allow to harden in the refrigerator for several hours before serving.

Michael Martin Cohen, M.D.

Shrimp Dip

Amy and I wouldn't think of celebrating New Year's Eve without this treat. Join us with this great dip.

⅓ cup cream or top milk
8 ounces cream cheese
2 teaspoons lemon juice

¼ teaspoon onion juice or fine
  gratings
3–4 drops Worcestershire sauce
4¾ ounces canned shrimp, drained

Just mix and serve.

Harold H. Payson

SNAPPER CRISPIAN

This appetizer is not the result of my passion for snapper, nor a dish I ate while in some exotic port. I just wanted to name something after my dog.

Makes 4 logs

1 package phyllo dough
6 tablespoons melted butter
1 pound red snapper,
  in ¼-inch strips

½ pound Stilton or Swiss cheese,
  or ¼ pound each, shredded
garlic powder, oregano, cumin
  to taste
grease for the pan

Lay the phyllo dough on a flat surface. Cover with a damp towel or plastic wrap to keep the leaves you are not working with from drying. To make a log, take a phyllo sheet, lay it flat, and brush with melted butter. Place another sheet on top of it, brush with butter, and repeat a third time. Cut the layered dough in half lengthwise. Arrange some strips of fish end-to-end lengthwise along the dough, leaving an inch or so on each side. Distribute about a fourth of the cheese over the fish and sprinkle well with spices. (A variety of flavor combinations can be used. The best ones are Swiss cheese, garlic, and cumin; Stilton and cumin *or* garlic *or* oregano; or simply Stilton.) Roll up the phyllo, seal the long edge with butter, press the ends to seal them, and place the roll, sealed edge down, on a greased cookie sheet. Make the other 3 logs in the same way and brush with remaining butter. If you are not going to bake the rolls right away, wrap them well in plastic. They can be refrigerated overnight, or frozen for up to 3 months.

Bake the logs uncovered, at 400 degrees for 20–25 minutes or until golden. Cut into 1–1½-inch lengths and serve hot. Each roll can be cut into about 10 pieces. Leftovers can be easily revived in a microwave oven or in a conventional oven at 350 degrees.

Lesley Newhart

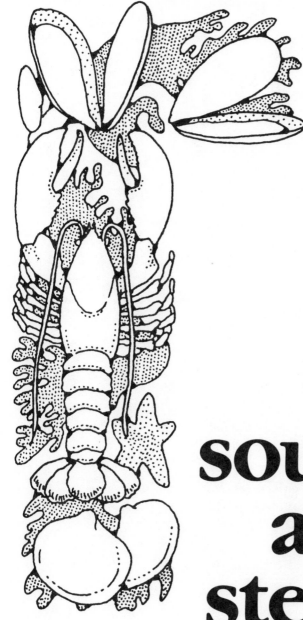

soups
and
stews

CLAM CHOWDER FOR 25

This chowder is rich and delicious. My wife makes this recipe for a crowd.

½ pound bacon, diced
2 large onions, chopped
3 large potatoes, diced (or 2 pounds
  frozen hash browns)
5 small cans minced clams and
  their juice

3 cans Snow's New England–style
  clam chowder
2 quarts half-and-half
1 stick butter
salt and pepper

Cook the bacon until crisp, drain, and set aside. In half the bacon grease sauté the onion slowly until transparent. Transfer to a large pot, adding the potatoes and juice from the clams. Simmer 15–20 minutes until the potatoes are soft, then mash them roughly with a spoon. Add the bacon, clams, clam chowder, half-and-half, and butter. Stir and season with salt and pepper. Heat to serve, being careful not to boil the chowder.

Richard Henderson

THOMAS TEW'S FISH CHOWDER

Having always been more adventurous at eating than cooking, I can say that the following chowder is the best I have found. The recipe has been maintained by my sister Esther Fisher Benson of Newport, Rhode Island, and goes back to Thomas Tew (same name as the pirate), a woodcarver who lived in Newport from 1818 to 1874. It may be complex, but what is said is true, and it is really very good.

Serves 10

3 four-pound blackfish
water to cover
¼ pound salt pork, sliced
1 quart onions, coarsely ground
1 quart potatoes, peeled and diced
1 quart canned tomatoes
1 lemon, washed and thinly sliced
water to cover

1¼ teaspoons poultry seasoning
    (sage, basil, marjoram, thyme)
½ teaspoon ground cloves
1 teaspoon sugar
a pinch of cayenne pepper
½ teaspoon black pepper
salt
1 cup red wine
1 tablespoon butter or margarine

Clean and scale the fish, leaving the head on, as the head contains good gelatin. Wrap the fish in cheesecloth, put in a deep pot, and cover with water. Simmer over a low fire until the fish is tender (allow 12 minutes to the pound). Remove the fish but leave the stock in the pot—there should be 3 quarts. Flake the fish from the bones. In a heavy iron skillet, fry the salt pork until golden. Add the pork to the stock, retaining the fat in the pan. Add the onion and fry until limp and pale gold. Add that to the stock. Rinse the frying pan with ½ cup stock to get every last bit of flavor and pour into the chowder. Add the potatoes and tomatoes. Simmer until potatoes are tender.

Prepare the lemon, discarding the tough ends. Quarter the slices, place in a saucepan, cover with water, and simmer slowly. After 10 minutes (do not let boil or the flavor will be bitter), add all the seasonings, stir a few times, and add the flaked fish. If you think more lemon is needed, add lemon juice to taste. Cook 10 minutes. Just before serving, add the wine and butter. Heat until very hot, but do not boil. Serve in deep bowls with pilot crackers.

Edward W. Smith, Jr.

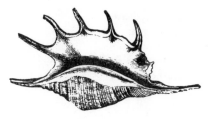

SEA BEAN STEW

Beans keep the sea well. They are easy to stow in big plastic containers and are full of natural protein.

1 cup red beans	2 potatoes
fresh water for boiling and soaking	2 large carrots
1 cup pearl barley	1 turnip
1 cup green lentils or split peas	1 can tomatoes
4 onions	1 tablespoon mixed herbs
1½ pints fresh water	1 teaspoon curry powder
1 cup salt water	2 vegetable-stock cubes

Boil red beans for 1 minute then soak in fresh water for 6 hours. Put beans, barley, lentils, and onions into a pressure cooker with the fresh and salt water. Bring to pressure and cook for 12 minutes. Reduce pressure, open cooker, and add the rest of the whole vegetables and seasonings. Bring back to pressure and cook another 8 minutes.

For second-day stew add 1 tin tuna fish. For third-day stew add more cooked vegetables and curry to taste.

Frank Mulville

Sea Bass Chowder

1 medium-sized sea bass
5 quarts water
3 large onions, sliced and quartered
½ cup cooking oil
3 eight-ounce cans tomato sauce
1 sixteen-ounce can stewed
   tomatoes

2 large bay leaves
1 cup vinegar
1 tablespoon salt
4 tablespoons Perfection-Brand
   crushed red peppers
2 carrots, sliced

Fillet the fish and set aside. Boil the remainder of the fish in the water for 30 minutes. Strain the broth into a clean container. In a separate kettle simmer the onions in the oil. Add all the other ingredients except carrots. Stir. Then add the carrots and broth and cook until carrots are almost tender. At the last, add the fish and simmer until done.

Allan H. Vaitses

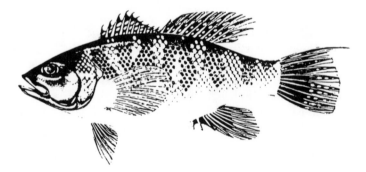

RHODE ISLAND CLAM CHOWDER

There are all sorts of clam chowders. Everyone I know turns up his or her nose at Manhattan clam chowder, since it has tomatoes. My side of the family always put milk in clam chowder, and my wife's side didn't. Except that my mother-in-law, if she were heating up some of my father-in-law's clam chowder and he didn't happen to be home, would add milk to his milkless chowder. Chowder prejudice is complicated.

Anyway, what you get here is my father-in-law's recipe for milkless clam chowder. I can attest to its excellence, even though I was brought up on clam chowder that had milk in it.

Serves 8

¼ pound lean salt pork, diced
4 tennis-ball-size onions, finely sliced
8 medium-sized potatoes, peeled, quartered, and sliced in wedges
1 quart clams and their juice (6 quarts in shell)
6 quarts hot water

In a big pot, fry the pork to a rich brown. Add the onion and cook until done. Remove the black from the clams' stomachs. Grind. Add the potatoes, ground clams and their juice, and 6 quarts hot water. Cook until the potatoes are done. (Wedge-shaped slices are important because the thin edges boil away and help to flavor the chowder.) Serve as-is for broth chowder or, if some prefer milk added, have a pitcher of warm milk at the table.

Roger C. Taylor

Old-Fashioned Fish Chowder

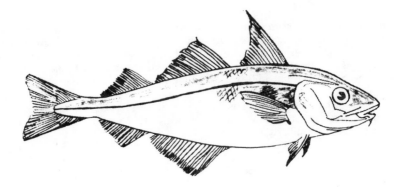

Serves 6–8 hungry people

1 onion, chopped
4 tablespoons margarine
4 potatoes, peeled and diced
water to cover
1½ pounds haddock

water to cover
1 large can evaporated milk
1 pint milk
salt and pepper
3 tablespoons butter

Sauté the onion in the margarine. Add the potatoes and just cover with water. Boil about 20 minutes. Add the fish and again cover with water. Cook another 20 minutes. Add the milks and simmer. Add salt, pepper, and butter.

Walter J. Simmons

CALLALOO

This is one I learned in Trinidad. It is tasty and exotic, and any reader going to the islands should try it. The callaloo bush, as the Trinidadians call it, looks like a small elephant's ear or taro. It is a close relative of those varicolored caladiums that add so much to any flower garden. In the tropics you will find bunches of callaloo (also known as dasheen, old cocoyam, and incorrectly as taro) growing around almost any country cottage. This recipe also provides a use for those great big, dark blue land crabs that you find everywhere in southern Florida and throughout the Caribbean. They are easy to locate because they make so much racket rattling around in the palmettos at night. Since they have claws that appear able to remove a finger with little effort, your best bet is to buy them in the marketplace: You will find them wired up with coconut fronds in bunches of a dozen, more or less. The evil look in their eyes should be warning enough to handle them with caution.

Serves 12, but 6 people can wipe out the whole pot if they are hungry

6–8 large blue land crabs (If none are available, the good folks in Trinidad use
    salt beef; our blue crabs or shrimp can serve as an excellent substitute.)
1 bunch callaloo greens
water
1 very large onion, chopped
1 coconut, grated, and its milk
16 large but not pithy okra, sliced in ½-inch chunks
boiled rice

Scald and clean the land crabs. Pick the leaves of the callaloo as you would do with any greens. The callaloo stems must be peeled, as with coarse celery. Put the callaloo stems and leaves into a large pot. Add about 2 inches of water. Bring to a gentle boil, stirring frequently. (The islanders use a special stirrer that looks like a stick with a spring wrapped on one end.) When the callaloo begins to get soft and slippery, add the onion. Continue to boil, and stir in the coconut and its milk. Add the cleaned crab bodies and claws. Then add the okra. Continue to cook for another half hour or longer, stirring frequently. Add water if necessary to keep the consistency of a thick stew. Serve over mounds of boiled rice, accompanied by boiled or baked plantains.

Warren Norville

MUSSEL SOUP

My family often braves icy New England waters as early as April and as late as November to get the mussels for this soup from below the low tide line. There is some truth to the rule of thumb that the tastiest seafood comes from the coldest waters.

Serves 4

2 garlic cloves
½ cup olive oil
2 tablespoons tomato sauce,
    preferably homemade
½ teaspoon salt

1 small bit of red pepper
3 dozen mussels in the shell,
    well scrubbed to remove sand
½ teaspoon oregano
8 one-inch slices of Italian bread

In a large pan brown 1 clove of garlic in the oil, then add the tomato sauce, salt, pepper, and mussels. Cook over a very high flame until all the mussels are open. Add the oregano and cook just a minute or so longer. Toast the bread and rub each slice with the second clove of garlic while still hot. Place 2 slices in each bowl, pour the mussels over them, and serve.

Paul Lipke

TUATUA SOUP

The tuatua is a fine New Zealand shellfish, similar to the clam and in this recipe interchangeable with any local shellfish.

Serves 4

3 tablespoons butter
3 tablespoons flour
3 cups hot milk
1 onion, finely chopped
garlic to suit your taste
1 teaspoon curry powder

1–2 cups minced tuatuas or clams
  (the more the better)
salt and pepper
1 cup dry white wine
chopped parsley

Melt the butter and add the flour to make a roux. Add the hot milk, stirring continuously, while allowing it to thicken. Add the onion, garlic, curry powder, and shellfish. Season with salt and pepper. Simmer 10 minutes. Just before serving, add the wine and garnish with parsley.

Eva Palasti Brown

CULLEN SKINK

An extremely tasty version of a Newfoundland chowder, this one, using smoked fish, is enjoyed by all the Hannas, including the ones who aren't fish-lovers.

Serves 4

1½–2 pounds finnan haddie or any
   thick, smoked fillet
water to cover
4 slices bacon
2 onions, coarsely chopped
4 cups potatoes, cubed or sliced

water to cover
1 can evaporated milk
a generous chunk of butter
salt and pepper
1 scant teaspoon sugar

Cover the fish with cold water and simmer for 2 minutes. Drain, reserving the liquid. Cook the bacon until crisp. Remove the slices and, when cool, crumble them for garnish. Transfer 2 tablespoons bacon fat to a large kettle. Add the onions and cook slowly until transparent. Add the potatoes, *some* of the fish stock (depending on strength of flavor), and water to cover. Place the fish on top of it all and simmer gently until the potatoes are tender and the fish flakes. Add the milk, butter, salt (if needed), pepper, and sugar and continue heating, stirring as little as possible. Do not allow the chowder to boil. It can be served at once, but is even better if allowed to mellow several hours at room temperature, then reheated slowly. Top each serving with crumbled bacon.

Jay S. Hanna

salads

SIMPLE SHRIMP STACKUPS

Serves 6

2 hard-boiled eggs
12 ounces shrimp, cooked and
   chopped
2 tablespoons chopped celery
2 tablespoons chopped sweet pickle
2 tablespoons thinly sliced
   green onion

½ cup plain yogurt
¼ cup cottage cheese
1 tablespoon lemon juice
a dash of pepper
lettuce leaves
12 tomato slices
6 toast slices, quartered

Chop the eggs, reserving 1 yolk. Cover and chill the reserved yolk. In a small bowl combine the shrimp, chopped egg, celery, pickle, and onion. In another bowl stir together the yogurt, cottage cheese, lemon juice, and pepper. Add this to the shrimp mixture, mix lightly, and chill. Prepare 6 individual lettuce-lined plates and place 2 tomato slices on each. Spoon about half a cup of the shrimp mixture on each plate. Sieve the reserved yolk atop each mound of shrimp. Accompany with toast quarters.

Pat Feener

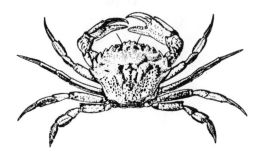

CRAB MOUSSE

1 cup cream	1 tablespoon boiling water
¾ cup mayonnaise	1 tablespoon gelatin
1 teaspoon thyme	4 tablespoons caviar
a pinch of salt	finely chopped parsley
a pinch of cayenne pepper	parsley sprigs and lettuce leaves
1 pound cooked crabmeat, flaked	

Blend the cream and mayonnaise in a mixing bowl. Add the thyme, salt, and pepper. Fold the crabmeat into the mayonnaise mixture. Pour the boiling water over the gelatin and stir until clear. Combine with the crab mixture. Rinse a mold in cold water. Place the mixture in the mold and chill until set. Unmold the mousse, place caviar and chopped parsley on top, and surround with parsley sprigs and lettuce.

Ross Norgrove

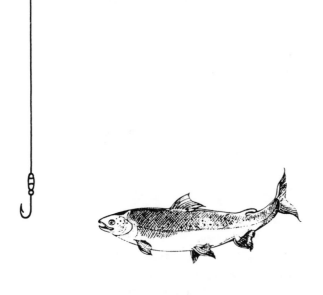

SALMON MOUSSE

Makes 4–5 servings or 10–12 appetizers

1 envelope plain gelatin	1 teaspoon minced dill
2 tablespoons lemon juice	2 cups cooked or 16 ounces
1 small onion, sliced	canned salmon
½ cup boiling water	1 cup plain yogurt
½ teaspoon paprika	

Pour the gelatin into a blender, add lemon juice, onion, and boiling water. Blend for 40 seconds. Add paprika, dill, and salmon. Blend briefly, then add the yogurt. Blend 30 seconds longer, pour into a mold, and chill. Unmold by placing in hot water for 45 seconds.

Jane Brooks

SHELLFISH SALAD

half a head of lettuce
1 can crabmeat
1 can lobster
1 can shrimp
6 radishes
1 avocado, diced

2 hard-boiled eggs, sliced
mayonnaise to taste
paprika
1 cucumber, peeled, marked
  with fork, and sliced

Break the lettuce up and place the pieces on a platter. Mix all the ingredients together except the cucumber. Place the mixture in a mound on the lettuce. Surround it with the cucumber slices. Sprinkle the top with paprika. Radish rosettes can be placed in the center for decoration.

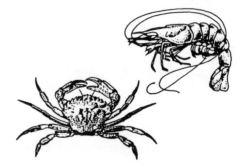

Wanda Clossey

MOLDED SHRIMP SALAD

Serves 8

1 tablespoon gelatin
2 tablespoons fresh lime or lemon
  juice
1½ cups hot water
½ teaspoon salt
½ teaspoon grated onion
¼ cup chili sauce
⅓ cup mayonnaise

1 avocado, halved, seeded,
  skinned, and diced
1¼ cups shrimp, cleaned and cooked
2 hard-cooked eggs, diced
¾ cup chopped celery
2 tablespoons chopped green pepper
black pepper
salad greens

Soften gelatin in lime or lemon juice and dissolve in hot water. Blend in salt, onion, and chili sauce. Cool to the consistency of unbeaten egg white. Blend in the mayonnaise. Fold the avocado, shrimp, egg, celery, green pepper, and black pepper into the gelatin mixture. Turn into individual molds and chill until firm. Unmold on salad greens to serve.

Linda Massey

Mark's Shrimp Salad For Heavy Eaters

The origin of this dates all the way back to 1978, when I was shamed into making a meal for a change. Not being familiar with stoves, I was forced to turn to another method of food preparation. This is a high-calorie salad for working folks—a complete meal in itself. The batch I made completely satiated 6 robust and very hungry adults. They were all impressed. So was I. Heart sufferers beware: This stuff has enough cholesterol in it to choke a horse.

Serves 6–18

½ pound alfalfa sprouts
12 large tomatoes, in chunks
½ pound sunflower seeds, roasted and lightly salted
1 pound almonds, roasted and cut in thirds
2 pounds raw cauliflower, cut in small segments (no leaves)
1 pound raw broccoli, sliced longitudinally into small pieces
    (don't use the thick stub ends)
7 avocados, cut in pieces
1½ pounds small mushrooms
¾ pound mild longhorn cheese, cut in ⅜-inch squares
2 heads romaine lettuce (Most folks say to tear the stuff up to maintain
    freshness, but I just slice it; it doesn't stay in the bowl very long anyway.)
2–4 pounds cooked shrimp
a dash of vinegar
a few sprigs of dill
a small handful of crushed bacon
generous amounts of sour cream or Marie's Ranch salad dressing

---

Into a large caldron go all the ingredients (except dressing), which you toss well because all the small stuff tends to slide to the bottom. Serve immediately with plenty of sour cream or salad dressing. This is a really filling meal.

Mark White

entrees

EAT IT ALL NOW!
OR
THE ART OF COOKING FRESH FISH

The primary ingredient of this recipe is time, and the quantity is "as little as humanly possible."

Much of the material for my book *The Case for the Cruising Trimaran* was gathered on a three-year family cruise of Central America (both sides). We were four in our thirty-one-foot cutter, *Scrimshaw*, with limited storage capacity and no refrigeration. Fresh food was a main concern, and we found that we were almost always able to catch something from the sea when we needed it.

Our seafood divided itself into two types, "swimming critters" and "crawling critters." The latter have the unique advantage of staying alive up to and including, if you wish, the time you are ready to eat them (witness "raw" or *live* oysters).

Swimming critters may decide to jump at the hook or swim in front of the spear at times other than mealtimes and, regrettably, that propensity terminates not only their vitality but also, as we finally realized, their absolute freshness. We learned that by *not* preparing swimming critters instantaneously a full 50 percent—yea even 51 percent—of their culinary grace and spiritual potency is dissipated elsewhere than to the consumer. Which is a complicated way to say that fresh fish is twice as good!

"Nothing new," you say. Well, wait a minute. No...don't wait, even a minute. Stop the boat, midmorning or midnight, fillet that finny friend while he's still flipping, and put on the pot. If it's the finest flavor you want, swimming critters should be enjoyed before they have the chance to rigor-mort. And certainly before they are allowed to come within a long arm's reach of refrigeration.

Of cooking methods, we investigated 50 and settled on two. The secret of both frying and poaching (we didn't have a broiler) appears to be this: Don't "cook" fresh fish. Just warm it all the way through, no warmer than 212 degrees. As you know, when water boils, it expands to about 1,700 times its liquid volume and is driven off as steam. So, if you "cook" your fish, its succulence is driven off with the steam, resulting in dry, compacted muscle fibers.

Poaching

fresh fish, no more than 1 inch thick
onion, in thick slices
water or milk to cover
seasoning
lemon or lime juice

Dress the fish. Cover the bottom of a large frying pan (one that has a lid) with onion, and place the fish on top. This holds the onion down and keeps the fish from touching the hot frying pan. Then nearly cover with water. If the fish is strong or oily, use milk—fresh, powdered, or (best of all) straight from the half-ripe coconut. Season, if you must. Try pepper alone or a few fennel seeds. Simmer, covered, until, when tested in the center of the largest piece with a fork, the fish pulls easily apart from itself or the backbone. A squirt of lemon or lime juice on each bite is essential for fighting scurvy.

Frying

fresh fish, no more than 1 inch thick
beaten egg
cracker crumbs
light vegetable oil
lemon juice

Dress the fish and dip in egg then cracker crumbs. Cornmeal or flour will work, but that tends to induce overcooking. Cracker crumbs will brown with much less heat, giving the true sign that the fish is done *before* it is overdone. Fry the fish in a little oil (not butter) and serve wrapped in paper towels to blot and keep warm. Don't ever allow the fresh fish to get really hot during cooking. Popping fat indicates too much heat. If through dreadful circumstance you must use fish that has been on ice, allow it to reach room temperature before frying and turn the pieces *before* your finger can feel the heat coming through the top of the thickest piece. Fry the second side a little hotter but for half the time. Again, lemon is essential to maintain the vigor of the crew.

Wine, no matter what the quality or color, leaves an unpleasant aftertaste when taken with delicate, exclusively fresh seafood, but Dos Equis Mexican beer is permissible.

That's enough dogma out of me—unless, of course, the reader is concerned with catching as well as cooking the fish, which is implied if the "swimmers" are ingested really fresh. Our trolling system is efficient but not sporty. We use hand trolling lines only 100 feet long but 500-pound test, with heavy wire leader (1/16-inch, 7x7, with Nicopress splices) and artificial lures. A big fish seems to require three fishermen: two to haul it in and the other to gaff and board it; then two to sit on it while the third pours a shot of gin directly into its gills. This is a far neater method of subduing a 40-pounder than stabbing it, clubbing it, or just letting it flop around in the cockpit, beating up the boat and covering everything with slime and scales and blood. In practice, we turn back the big boys unless we're headed for harbor, where most of the meat can be given away. Tantalizing as a four-foot tuna or mahimahi may be, it's really only half as good as a four-pound sierra mackerel (our favorite) because with a big fish and a small crew you simply cannot eat it all *now*!

Jim Brown

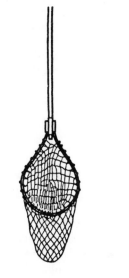

LEMON-CURRIED SHRIMP AND TOMATOES

Serves 4

2 pounds jumbo shrimp
¼ cup lemon juice, freshly squeezed
⅓ cup cider vinegar
1 teaspoon cumin
1 teaspoon turmeric
½ teaspoon cayenne pepper
½ teaspoon black pepper,
   freshly ground
4 teaspoons salt
¼ cup vegetable oil
1 teaspoon black mustard seeds

2 tablespoons fresh ginger root,
   scraped and finely chopped
1 tablespoon garlic, finely chopped
1 cup onions, finely chopped
6 ripe tomatoes, coarsely chopped
2 tablespoons dark brown sugar
½ teaspoon dark molasses
3 tablespoons fresh coriander,
   finely chopped
3 tablespoons hot green chili,
   chopped and seeded

Carefully shell the shrimp, leaving the last segment of the shell and the tail attached. Devein the shrimp, then rinse under cold running water and pat dry. To make the marinade, combine the lemon juice, vinegar, cumin, turmeric, cayenne pepper, black pepper, and 3 teaspoons of the salt. Add the shrimp and marinate at room temperature for about half an hour.

Heat the oil in a heavy skillet over moderate heat. Stir in the mustard seeds, ginger, garlic, onions, and the last teaspoon of salt. Stirring constantly, sauté the onions until soft and golden brown. Do not let them burn. Drain the marinade, but not the shrimp, into the skillet. Add the tomatoes and stir for 3 minutes. Mix the brown sugar and molasses. Sprinkle in the coriander, then drop in the shrimp, coating them on all sides. Sprinkle the chili on top, partially cover the skillet, and cook for 3 minutes or until the shrimp are pink and firm. Serve at once.

Nan Kulikauskas

DEEP-FRIED SCALLOPS

Serves 3 (hungry) or 4

½ cup flour
½ teaspoon salt
1 pound scallops
1 egg

3 tablespoons milk
fine cracker crumbs
oil for frying

In a paper bag, mix the flour and salt, add the scallops, and shake to coat. In a bowl, beat the egg and the milk. Have the cracker crumbs ready in another container. Completely coat the floured scallops in the egg mixture, then in crumbs. Deep-fry in oil until golden brown. If you have to use a small fryer, fry a few at a time and keep them warm in an oven until all are ready to serve.

Howard Barnes

BAKED SCALLOPS

Very good on a cold winter's night.

scallops
flour
grease for the pan

milk to cover
dots of butter
salt and pepper

Wash the scallops and remove the ears (the hard pieces). Dry the scallops well and roll each one in flour. Place in a greased pie pan or casserole dish. Fill the dish about half full with milk. Dot the scallops with butter. Add salt and pepper to taste. Bake at 350 degrees for 30 minutes, then turn the scallops and brown them on the other side. Serve at once.

Walter J. Simmons

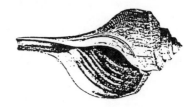

MARY BARTHOLOMEW'S ROLLUPS

Mary Bartholomew, a West Indian, was the Hendersons' cook when they lived on the island of Grenada during 1967–1968.

Serves 4

½ stick butter
½ onion, diced
¼ cup diced green pepper
1 pound cleaned shrimp or cut-up
   West Indian lobster tail
¼ cup bread crumbs
1 tablespoon minced parsley
½ teaspoon salt

⅛ teaspoon pepper
8 sole, lemon sole, or flounder
   fillets
2 tablespoons butter
melted butter for the top
the juice of 1 lemon
1 stick butter

Melt ½ stick butter in a large skillet, stir in the onion and green pepper, and cook slowly until the onion is clear. Put in the shrimp and cook briefly. Remove about half the shrimp and put aside. Mince the rest. Mix with the bread crumbs, parsley, salt, pepper, onions, and green pepper. Spread about 2 tablespoons of this mixture on each fish fillet. Then roll up the fillets and place flap side down in a shallow baking dish in which 2 tablespoons butter have been melted. Tuck any remaining stuffing into the ends of the rollups. Brush the tops with melted butter. Bake at 350 degrees for 20 minutes. At the last minute heat the rest of the shrimp in lemon-butter sauce. Make this by heating the lemon juice and 1 stick butter and stirring until well mixed. Pour over the rollups and serve.

Richard Henderson

SOUTH COUNTY PIE

The "South County" in the name of this dish is the South County of Rhode Island. Because oysters are involved, the thing is sometimes known as Chesapeake Pie. It's good with Chesapeake oysters, but it's better with oysters out of Charlestown Pond, in the heart of the South County.

This is my favorite seafood dish and is the only one I've mastered as far as the cooking part goes. I know a lady who the first time she ate South County Pie exclaimed, "Owww! This is so good it hurts!"

Serves 4 people with good appetites

1 pint oysters
2 cups Bisquick
1 pound link sausages

First, round up a 6 x 9-inch baking dish to make the best depth for the finished pie. Then, drain the oysters and place them in the bottom of the baking dish. Using the shortcake recipe on the Bisquick box, mix the Bisquick with all the specified ingredients except sugar until it becomes a sticky mass. Spread the batter evenly over the oysters, then lay the sausage links close together, half burying them in the dough. Bake at 375 degrees for 45 minutes or until the biscuit dough is done. It needs no other seasoning than the sausage and oysters. Serve with a tossed salad. (Know your sausage: If it is quite greasy, fry out some of the fat first in a skillet. Too much grease and the dough will not bake like a biscuit but will be a soft puddingy mass.)

Roger C. Taylor

RHODE ISLAND CLAM BAKE

This is my father-in-law's recipe. People have different ideas about clambakes, and as you can see from the note about the lobsters, Grampa changed his mind about this one.

This bake is not just a meal. It's a gala event. We're talking here about giving up an entire day. And it's best to plan to sleep near the site.

Serves 18

16 quarts soft-shell steamer clams	melted butter
water to cover	18 lobsters
3 tablespoons vinegar	1 bushel rockweed from clean salt
18 potatoes in their jackets	water
18 ears of sweet corn on the cob	1 large potato
18 flounder fillets	1 quart water
36 link sausages	

About 4 hours before baking time, cover the clams with water, add the vinegar, and stir well. This makes the clams throw off sand and does not alter their taste. Scrub the potatoes, leaving the skins on. Husk and desilk the corn, removing all but the innermost layer. Roll each fillet around 2 sausages, then wrap the fillets in patapar paper. Divide the steamers in thirds and put each portion in a gauze bag for ease in removing from the bake.

For the cooking, use a large, heavy-duty metal refuse can, with its cover, over an open grate or an improvised fireplace made of cinder blocks. Devise a rack about 4 inches high that will raise the bake above the juices. Pack in this order (which makes it come in the right order for serving): layer of rockweed, live lobsters, rockweed, fish-and-sausage packages, rockweed, sweet corn, rockweed, potatoes, rockweed, bags of clams, rockweed. This fills the can. In the top layer of rockweed bury the large potato as a timer. Put the quart of water in the can, cover it, and set it over the fireplace. Make a brisk fire underneath, and keep the fire going until the bake is done. Note when steam begins to come out around the cover: Approximately 1 hour and 10 minutes from this time the bake should be done. But if the potato on top is not well done, cook awhile longer until it is. Remove the can from the fire.

Each course should be served hot to be best.

First course: Clams served with melted butter.

Second course: Potatoes, sweet corn, and the fish-and-sausage rolls.

Third course: Lobsters served with melted butter. Each lobster should be split open and the claws given a breaking crack to make it easier to get the meat out.

NOTE: Experience has taught that the lobster gets overcooked if put at the bottom of the bake, so put the lobster on top. When unpacking the bake, put the lobsters between two layers of hot rockweed to keep them warm for serving last.

Roger C. Taylor

Quahog Pie

2 cups quahogs, finely chopped	1 onion, sliced and gently fried
1½ cups of their liquor	¼ cup flour
1 two-inch cube salt pork, finely diced	enough pie dough for 2 large crusts
	3 raw potatoes, thinly sliced

In a skillet mix the quahogs, their liquor, salt pork, onion, the fat it was fried in, and flour. Simmer 20 minutes. Line a large pie plate with the unbaked crust, then about a third of the potatoes. Add half the quahog mixture, another layer of potatoes, the rest of the mixture, the last layer of potatoes, and the top crust. Cook slowly for 2 hours, and enjoy the very finest kind of quahog pie.

Phil Schwind

CRAB EDDIE

Serves 10

2 pounds backfin crabmeat	1 pound mushrooms, sliced and
2 cups mayonnaise	sautéed
2 cups half-and-half	4 hard-cooked eggs, diced
2 tablespoons chopped onion	1 package Pepperidge Farm stuffing
2 tablespoons chopped parsley	dots of butter

Mix all ingredients except half the stuffing and the butter. Put in a casserole dish, top with the rest of the stuffing, and dot with butter. Bake at 350 degrees for 40 minutes.

Linda Massey

CRAB IMPERIAL

2 pounds crabmeat	2 tablespoons minced parsley
2 raw eggs	4 teaspoons Worcestershire sauce
3 slices stale white bread,	4 tablespoons mayonnaise
finely crumbled	salt, pepper, dry mustard
3 tablespoons minced pimiento	extra mayonnaise thinned with
3 tablespoons minced green pepper	cream for topping

Combine all ingredients except the topping. Put in a casserole dish and top with the thinned mayonnaise. Bake in a moderate oven (350 degrees) until brown.

Linda Massey

COCONUT CRAB CURRY

Serves 4–6

1 fresh coconut, coarsely chopped
3 tablespoons coriander seeds
2½ cups hot, not boiling, water
¼ cup vegetable oil
12 whole black peppercorns
1 garlic clove, peeled and slightly crushed
1 one-inch piece fresh ginger root, scraped and slightly crushed
½ cup finely chopped onions
1 teaspoon salt
½ teaspoon ground coriander
¼ teaspoon ground cumin
¼ teaspoon turmeric
a pinch of cayenne pepper
4 tablespoons fresh coriander, finely chopped
1 pound crabmeat, picked clean

Blend the coconut with the coriander seeds and 1 cup hot water in an electric blender at high speed until the mixture is reduced to a purée. Line a fine sieve with a double thickness of dampened cheesecloth and set it over a bowl. Pour in the purée. Gather the ends of the cheesecloth together and squeeze out as much coconut milk as possible. There should be about 1¼ cups. Set aside. Return the coconut pulp to the blender, add the remaining 1½ cups of hot water, and blend for 30 seconds. Repeat the process of squeezing the milk through the cheesecloth, only squeeze it into a separate bowl. There should be 1–1½ cups of the second coconut milk. Discard the pulp.

Heat the oil over moderate heat in a heavy 2- to 3-quart saucepan. Add the peppercorns, garlic, and ginger. Stir for 30 seconds. Add the onions and salt and sauté until soft and golden brown. Add the ground coriander, cumin, turmeric, and cayenne pepper. Stir 2–3 minutes. Pour in the second coconut milk and bring to a boil over high heat. Reduce the heat to low, partially cover, and simmer for 10 minutes. Remove the lid and raise the heat to high. While stirring constantly with one hand, use the other to slowly pour in a thin stream of the first coconut milk. Add 2 tablespoons of the fresh coriander and all the crabmeat. Cook briskly for 2–3 minutes to heat the crab, then remove from the heat. Sprinkle in the remaining coriander, cover the pan tightly, and let the curry steep for 5 minutes before serving.

Nan Kulikauskas

BOILED SHRIMP

Despite all the ways to fix shrimp, there is no better way than simply to boil them. Allow half a pound of shrimp per person, heads off (about ¾ pound, heads on). Shrimp have a better flavor if boiled with their heads on. When cooking any shellfish, it is important to cook them only the barest minimum required to get them done. When we have a large gang of folks together, we cook about two-thirds of the shrimp as described. The other third we season with cayenne pepper to make the dish quite piquant.

Serves 10

7 pounds shrimp with the heads on (5 pounds, heads off)
water to cover
1 lime or lemon, sliced
2 fresh bay leaves (if not available, use 2 dried from your own tree and, as a
    last resort, 4 from the store)
1 tablespoon salt
1 teaspoon black pepper
1 teaspoon liquid crab and shrimp boil (may vary to individual taste)
3 dashes Louisiana hot sauce or a pinch of cayenne pepper (optional)
2 tablespoons Worcestershire sauce

Thoroughly rinse the shrimp, drain, and set aside. Fill a boiling pot with enough water to cover the shrimp (which are not yet in the pot) about 1 inch. Dump in the rest of the ingredients, stir, and bring to a rolling boil. At that point, add the shrimp. As soon as the water boils again, take the pot off the stove and drain the shrimp in a colander, saving the water for later use as gumbo stock. Serve the shrimp either hot or chilled.

An alternate method especially good with larger shrimp is to place them in the pot with the other ingredients and cover with an inch or so of cold water. Place on high heat. The instant the water begins to boil, remove the pot from the stove and drain as above. Some good with beer! Let your crew head and peel their own. It's part of the fun.

Warren Norville

UM-GOOD MACKEREL

Trolling for mackerel is great sport along the Maine coast from June through September. The only way to eat mackerel is flipping fresh. This is a recipe the Indians used on Penobscot Bay. It was written down on a piece of birch bark and handed along through the Brown generations.

as many mackerel as you care to eat   salt water
driftwood planks   nails
big gobs of clay

When enough fish have been caught, pull ashore at a Maine island. Plenty to choose from. Clean the fish. Divide the catch in half: Split half up the middle and leave half in the round. Gather the driftwood and dig the clay from intertidal areas (flats). Mix the clay with the salt water until it is like putty. Coat the fish-in-the-round ½ inch thick with clay and set aside to dry a little. Build a fire. Nail the split fish onto the planks, skin side down. Or, if you have no nails, split the planks down from the top and insert the split fishes' tails in the crack. Set the planks close to the fire, propping them up vertically. Throw the clayed fish straight into the fire. The planked fish, which are your immediate dinner, will be ready when the meat is all brown and crispy. Great with beer. A couple of hours later, clean the area whistle clean, kick the rock-hard clay-coated fish from the fire, and thoroughly extinguish the coals. Put the clayed fish in a metal bucket. They can be cracked like walnuts and eaten the rest of the day at leisure or taken home for supper, as they stay warm for 6 hours. The skin comes off with the clay, exposing the steamy, moist, white meat inside.

Mike Brown

BAKED FRESH SALMON

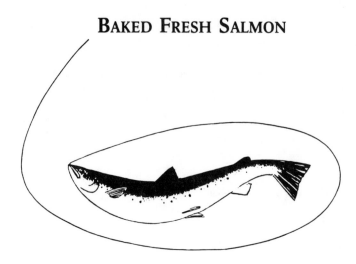

Before sailing our *Gabbiano* back to the United States, Martha and I spent four weeks in the summer of 1974 cruising Norway's great fjords north of Bergen. Returning from Geirangerfjord, and bound for Alesund and the Norwegian Sea, we spent a night anchored off the steep shore of Storfjord at the village of Siljenes. The chill of the dark and rainy evening was broken when Mr. Cato Normann of Oslo, who summered in those northern waters, came alongside with a 22-inch salmon that he had just caught. Following his instructions, I cleaned the fish immediately and stored it in the cold pilothouse overnight where the seagulls could not reach it. Martha cooked it for dinner the next day according to this recipe, which she created with the stores on board.

---

1 fresh salmon
water to cover
2 cans cream of celery soup
1 soup can Hvitvin or another
  dry white wine

2 tablespoons dried basil
3 hard-boiled eggs, chopped
slabs of Jarlsberg or another
  mild cheese

Boil the salmon for 20 minutes and set aside. Mix together the soup, wine, basil, and chopped egg. Pour the mixture over the salmon. Top with cheese and bake in a moderate oven for about 40 minutes or until the top has browned.

Brainerd Chapman

MARYLAND CRAB CAKES

There is no seafood delicacy superior to the Chesapeake Bay blue crab. The best way to partake, of course, is to eat the choice morsels as you open the shell! This is a bit messy, however, so for a more formal dining atmosphere, many Marylanders prefer crab cakes.

Serves 4

1 pound crabmeat, backfin preferred	1 teaspoon dry mustard
½ cup Miracle Whip salad dressing	salt and pepper
3 tablespoons chopped green pepper	dry cracker or bread crumbs
1 tablespoon chopped onion	cooking oil
2 tablespoons chopped pimiento	fresh parsley
2 eggs	lemon juice
2 teaspoons Worcestershire sauce	

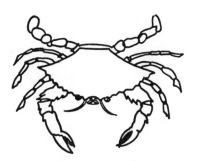

In a bowl, mix the crab, dressing, chopped vegetables, eggs, and seasonings. Make small patties and roll them in crumbs. Fry in a lightly oiled pan, just a few minutes on each side until lightly browned. Garnish with fresh parsley and serve with lemon juice.

This same mixture may also be made into Crab Imperial by omitting 1 egg. Pile the mixture into individual scallop shells or casserole dishes and bake at 325 degrees for 30 minutes.

G.D. Dunlap

BROILED OYSTERS

Before anything else, a few comments about oysters. Oysters are best if opened immediately before using. Fortunately they are excellent if opened several days before using, and kept refrigerated. To realize a quart of oysters for the galley, I need to open one of those big shrimp baskets (the 83-pound size). Such a basket holds more than a gallon of oysters, but the attrition rate is awful, trying to get them past my gaping maws and those of my audience as I open them. Before you buy oysters ask, "Are they salty?" If the answer is, "They're fresh," try to find some salty ones. There is no way you can fix oysters that begins to compare with good salty oysters, fresh off the shell. NEVER WASH OYSTERS. It ruins the flavor of raw ones and doesn't help the flavor of the cooked ones. If you open oysters carefully and set them in a coarse sieve, most of the shell and grit will settle to the bottom. Always save the oyster liquor for soups, stews, and gumbos. Just in case you could not eat them all raw, here's how you broil oysters.

A light entree for 4 or appetizer for 6

½ stick butter or margarine
1 quart oysters, unwashed and drained
½ teaspoon Italian seasoning
¼ cup dry vermouth, dry sherry, or
   another dry wine
1 large garlic toe (I use 2–3),
   finely chopped

½ teaspoon salt (vary if oysters
   are very salty)
NO PEPPER!
toasted slices of French or
   Italian bread

Heat a large iron skillet over moderately high heat. Melt the butter. When melted, pour in the drained oysters. If the oysters make too much liquid, drain it off and save it: The oysters should only be about one-fourth covered. Cook over moderate to high heat for 3–4 minutes or until the edges of the oysters begin to curl. Add the Italian seasoning, garlic, and salt and stir. Pour in the vermouth. When the vermouth shows the first sign of boiling, remove the pan from the heat. Cover and let stand for a few minutes. Serve over the toasted bread with a bottle of chilled soave blanco.

This recipe can be varied with the addition of pepper, different seasonings, and Worcestershire sauce (1 tablespoon, not ¼ cup) instead of wine. To oven-broil, put the oysters in a large pan so none are on top of each other. Put them under a broiler. Two or three minutes later, pull them out, stir them, and run them back in. As soon as they begin to shrivel and curl slightly around the edges, take them out, pour on the vermouth, and continue as directed above.

Warren Norville

CREAMED OYSTERS AND SHRIMP— OLD-LONG-ISLAND STYLE

Serves 6

1 pint oysters	a dash of cayenne pepper
1 cup shrimp	1 cup light cream
½ cup sherry	2 beaten egg yolks
½ stick melted butter	2 tablespoons brandy
1½ tablespoons flour	toast or patty shells
½ teaspoon salt	

Heat the oysters and drain. Cook the shrimp and separate into small pieces. Add to oysters. Pour in the sherry and let stand 1 hour. Transfer to a saucepan, add the butter, and cook for 5 minutes over low fire. Sprinkle the seafood with the flour, salt, and pepper and cook for 2 or 3 minutes. Add the cream and, when thickened, add the egg yolks and brandy. Serve at once on toast or patty shells.

Eleanor Stephens
(daughter of W.P. Stephens)

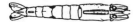

West Branch Trout

There was a time when I embarked upon the waterways of Maine for an extended canoe trip very lightly provisioned. The reasoning behind such ventures was a totally unfounded confidence in my ability to supplement the wanigan with food sources available naturally. Well, sometimes there was very little available, or at least I couldn't turn up much, and the fare on these trips was both meager and monotonous. Thank God I have gotten that nonsense out of my system, and nowadays I never set foot in the woods without provisions enough to last twice as long as the intended outing.

Still, there are times when Mother Nature is unusually generous with her bounty and I am fortunate enough to catch a few nice trout. If by coincidence I am along a fine stream like the West Branch and the wild chives are in season, I prepare the fish at the first available campsite.

For each serving:

1 12–14-inch brook trout,
  gutted and rinsed
3 teaspoons flour
1 teaspoon salt

1 teaspoon pepper, freshly ground
2 tablespoons cooking oil
a small fistful of wild chives

Start a brisk campfire with enough dry wood to create a good hot bed of coals when the flames dwindle. Place the trout with the head still attached into a paper sack containing the flour, salt, and pepper and shake until the fish is thoroughly coated. Heat the oil in the heavy camp frying pan until it is good and warm. Dice the wild chives into the oil, covering the bottom of the pan. Sauté. Lay the trout on top of the chives and cook gently, turning frequently until the skin is golden brown and the meat breaks easily away from the backbone.

When cooking fresh trout at home, substitute 4 small shallots for the wild chives and serve with a lemon wedge.

Jerry Stelmok

QUICK CODFISH CURRY

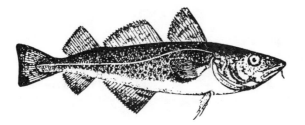

This recipe is not only easy to fix, but easy on the calories too—only 144 per serving!

Serves 6

¼ cup honey	1 teaspoon salt
¼ cup Dijon-style mustard	1½ pounds ¾-inch cod or other
2 tablespoons lemon juice	whitefish fillets
2 teaspoons curry powder	snipped chives and parsley

In a bowl combine the first five ingredients. Place the fish in a shallow dish. Spread about half the honey mixture over the fish; then turn and brush with the rest. Let stand 15 minutes. Reserving the marinade, place the fish on the rack of a broiler pan and broil 4 inches from the heat for 10–12 minutes. Brush occasionally with some of the marinade, and keep the rest warm to pass at the table. Remove the fish from the oven, place on a platter, and top with snipped chives and parsley. To prepare in a microwave oven, cook the curry in a covered dish on the "high" setting for 8–11 minutes, turning the dish and basting the fish with marinade 2–3 times.

Pat Feener

SHRIMP GREEK STYLE

Serves 4

6 tablespoons olive oil
¼ cup onions, finely chopped
1 twelve-ounce can tomatoes,
   chopped and drained
½ cup dry white wine
1 tablespoon Italian parsley,
   finely chopped
½ teaspoon oregano

½ teaspoon dill
½ teaspoon salt
cracked black pepper to taste
1 pound frozen shrimp, thawed
   quickly in boiling water
1 teaspoon capers
2 ounces feta cheese, crumbled

Heat the oil in a skillet or flameproof casserole dish. Add the onions and cook until soft, about 5 minutes. Stir in the tomatoes, wine, parsley, oregano, dill, salt, and pepper. Bring to a boil and cook until mixture begins to thicken. Add shrimp and cook over medium heat for no more than 2 minutes. Add capers. Add cheese and taste. Serve immediately over rice pilaf.

Kathleen Brandes

LOBSTER À LA MININE

For each serving:

The Lobster:
1 live lobster
salt and pepper
2 eggs, slightly beaten
fine bread crumbs
butter for the pan

The Sauce:
4 tablespoons butter
1 large onion, sliced
1 lime or ½ a large lemon
flour and water
seasonings
hot sauce
parsley sprigs

Buy or catch your lobster (and we're sorry about this, but it has to be alive). Crack the shell with whatever is handy—I once did it with a bottle of Mount Gay rum. Remove the meat with a sharp knife and cut it into mouth-sized pieces (depends upon the size of your mouth). Add the salt and pepper to the beaten eggs. Dip the lobster pieces in the egg, then in bread crumbs, and fry them in butter. Do not overcook. For the sauce, melt the butter, add the onion, then squeeze in the juice of the lime or lemon. Add flour and water to make a medium-thick sauce. Season to taste. Stir in hot sauce if desired. Pour the sauce over the lobster and garnish with parsley.

Ross Norgrove

 # HOME-AT-LAST CLAMS

A hundred years ago when Cap'n Caleb Drinkwater returned from a three-year whaling voyage, he told the Missus he craved three things—fresh clams, fresh milk, and fresh eggs. She obliged—hence the name of this century-old Saturday Cove recipe.

---

4 servings with no leftovers

2 cups whole milk
2 cups crumbled salt crackers
1 pint fresh clams, cut up real small, and their juice
  (You could use 2 seven-ounce cans of store-bought minced clams, but
  Caleb would turn over in his you-know-what.)
4 eggs, well beaten
¼ cup minced onion
¼ teaspoon black pepper
a couple pats of butter
grease for the pan

Pour the milk over the crumbled crackers and let stand 20 minutes. Add the other stuff, including clam juice but not the butter, and mix lightly. Pour into a greased bread tin or casserole dish, top with butter, and bake at 350 degrees for about 45 minutes or until firm.

Mike Brown

GREEN FETTUCINE WITH SCALLOP AND PARSLEY SAUCE

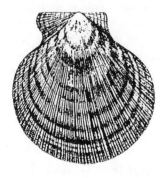

Serves 6

½ cup fresh parsley, minced
1 shallot, minced
6 tablespoons butter
½ cup dry white wine
¾ pound sea scallops, sliced into
   ¼-inch rounds
1 cup half-and-half

½ cup heavy cream
1 cup grated Parmesan cheese
nutmeg, salt, pepper
1½ pounds green fettucine
water to cover
1 teaspoon capers
parsley sprigs and extra Parmesan

Cook ¼ cup of the parsley and the shallot in 4 tablespoons butter over moderate heat, stirring, for 5 minutes or until shallot is softened. Add wine and reduce mixture to about 6 tablespoons over moderately high heat, stirring. Add scallops and continue stirring for 1 minute. Add half-and-half and cream. Simmer 2 minutes. Remove from heat. Stir in the 1 cup Parmesan, nutmeg, salt, pepper, and the remaining ¼ cup parsley. Add capers. Set sauce aside and keep warm.

Cook fettucine in boiling, oiled, salted water until *al dente*. Drain and toss with the remaining 2 tablespoons butter. Spoon sauce over fettucine. Serve with parsley garnish and extra Parmesan.

Nan Kulikauskas

SHRIMP CASSEROLE

Bound northward from Florida to Maine in the spring of 1980, we called at Charleston, South Carolina, to see relatives, including our niece, Mary Jane Edwards, of Columbia, South Carolina. A celebrated cook and hostess, Janie is sometimes asked to prepare menus for state dinners in the governor's mansion. My wife, Martha, contemplating fresh fish on our trip north, asked Janie for some recipes. This is one of her own making.

Serves 10–12

The Shrimp:
5 pounds raw shrimp in their shells
   (3 pounds raw shrimp, shelled)
water to cover
salt, bay leaf, and a touch of
   vinegar

The Seasoned Butter:
1 stick butter
2 teaspoons Worcestershire sauce
1 garlic clove, chopped
¼ cup fresh parsley, chopped
¼ cup chives or green onion
   tops, chopped
salt and pepper

The Sauce:
⅓ cup butter
3 tablespoons flour
½ teaspoon salt
a touch of pepper
1½ cups shrimp stock
   (as prepared below)
3 teaspoons lemon juice, or more,
   to taste

The Topping:
2 handfuls grated sharp
   Cheddar cheese
buttered bread crumbs

Put the shrimp in boiling, salted water. Add the salt, bay leaf, and vinegar and cook for only a short time: The shrimp should be *undercooked*. Drain the shrimp and save the stock. Clean the shrimp and put them aside. Melt the stick of butter and stir in the seasonings. Cook for a short time, then remove from the heat. Add the shrimp and set aside. Blend the ingredients for the sauce and cook 5 minutes. Combine the shrimp mixture and the sauce in a shallow casserole dish. Top with sharp Cheddar, then sprinkle the bread crumbs over the cheese. Bake at 350 degrees until heated through.

Brainerd Chapman

CRAB CASSEROLE

5 tablespoons flour
½ stick butter
½ teaspoon salt
⅛ teaspoon pepper
¼ teaspoon dry mustard

2 tablespoons Worcestershire sauce
2 cups milk
¾ cup grated sharp Cheddar cheese
1 pound backfin crabmeat
1 slice fresh bread, finely crumbled

In the top of a double boiler, whisk together the first 6 ingredients. Slowly add milk and whisk frequently until sauce is thick. Add the grated cheese and cook until melted. Add the crabmeat. Put the mixture in a casserole dish and top with bread crumbs. Bake at 350 degrees for 30 minutes.

Linda Massey

CRABMEAT PIE

Excellent!

½ cup mayonnaise
½ cup milk
2 eggs
2 tablespoons flour

8 ounces crabmeat
4 ounces shredded Swiss cheese
chopped onions to taste
1 nine-inch unbaked pie shell

Beat together the mayonnaise, milk, eggs, and flour. Then stir in the crabmeat, cheese, and onions. Pour into the pie shell and bake at 350 degrees for 40 minutes.

April Jenkins

SEA SCALLOPS FOR BREAKFAST

I suppose this recipe is not too practical for a great many people, although it's the proper way to eat sea scallops. Too often this choice shellfish comes too tired to the table. If you can buy scallops fresh off the boat, by all means do so. If frozen, thaw them first, then rinse them thoroughly in salted water. Dry on a paper towel and break off the hard little crescent on the narrow edge. Throw it away or feed it to your cat who, if she's a proper Cape Cod cat, will love it raw. Cut or break each scallop vertically into about four pieces and fry, broil, or bake as you would Cape or bay scallops.

Serves 2

1 thirty-eight-foot boat rigged for dragging with a six-foot "snow-plow" drag
a good-sized chunk of Canadian bacon
the resulting half or full bushel of deep-sea scallops

Take your boat and a crew of two. Run to Dennis Ledge in Cape Cod Bay and fish the afternoon out, sea-scalloping. When it gets too dark to see, work the drag warp over the bow and lay on the drag all night. After an uneasy night with all the creakings, rattlings, bangings, and sloshings that are a part of such a night, the first man up should fire up the machinery.

The helper should stoke the Shipmate stove in the cabin, put on a heavy iron skillet, and whittle into it several thick slices of Canadian bacon. The coffee pot, wired to the stove so it can't tip over, should be replenished with a handful of coffee and quart or so of water.

By the time the bacon is done and the coffee is almost boiled, the first tow should come aboard—a half or maybe a full bushel of scallops. One by one these deep-sea scallops should be shucked out of their shells and into the smoking-hot bacon fat in the frying pan until the bottom of the pan is covered. The scallops must quiver as they go into the fat or they are not really fresh.

Now, if the skipper insists on dragging while you eat your breakfast, let him run the boat, for he is hardly human. When the scallops are fried really hot, they should be bailed out into the biggest scallop shells of the first tow. Garnish with well-done bacon and wash down with hot, strong black coffee. (Throw overboard the shells you used for breakfast plates—you'll get more tomorrow.)

Phil Schwind

CURRIED COCONUT JUMBO SHRIMP

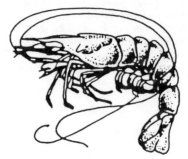

Serves 4–6

1 pound jumbo shrimp	½ cup onions, finely chopped
1 tablespoon vinegar	1 teaspoon turmeric
2 teaspoons salt	½ teaspoon cumin
1 cup coconut, coarsely chopped	¼ teaspoon cayenne pepper
¼ cup coriander seeds	¼ teaspoon black pepper,
1¼ cups warm water	freshly ground
5 tablespoons vegetable oil	3 tablespoons fresh coriander,
1 tablespoon fresh ginger root,	finely chopped
scraped and finely chopped	boiled rice
1 tablespoon garlic, finely chopped	

Carefully shell the shrimp, leaving the last segment of the shell and the tail attached. Devein the shrimp, then rinse under cold running water and pat dry. Combine the vinegar and salt, add the shrimp, and marinate at room temperature for 20 minutes.

Blend the coconut with the coriander seeds and water in an electric blender at high speed until reduced to a purée. Line a fine sieve with a double layer of damp cheesecloth and set it over a bowl. Pour in the purée. Gather the ends of the cheesecloth together and squeeze out as much coconut milk as possible: There should be about 1½ cups. Discard the pulp.

Heat 3 tablespoons of oil in a heavy skillet over moderate heat until a drop of water sizzles as soon as it hits the oil. Transfer each shrimp from the marinade to the skillet, cover tightly, and cook for 30 seconds. Turn the shrimp over, cover, and cook until pink and firm. Return the shrimp to the marinade.

Heat the remaining 2 tablespoons of oil. Add the ginger and stir for 30 seconds. Add the garlic and stir for 1 minute. Sauté the onions until soft and golden brown. Add the turmeric, cumin, cayenne pepper, and black pepper. Stir for 1 minute. Holding back the shrimp, pour the marinade into the skillet. Scrape the pan and immediately bring the liquid to a boil over high heat. Stirring constantly, add the coconut milk and shrimp. Bring to a boil. Reduce the heat, sprinkle with 2 tablespoons coriander, replace the lid, and cook for 3 minutes.

Transfer the contents of the skillet to a serving dish, sprinkle with the rest of the coriander, and serve with boiled rice.

Nan Kulikauskas

POTTED SHRIMP

1 pint shrimp per person	a good pinch of mace
2 tablespoons butter per pint	a dash of black pepper

Shell the shrimp. Melt the butter, then mix in the mace and pepper—no salt. Stir the shrimp into the seasoned butter, then pack them down into some sort of container. Cover them with foil and put something fairly heavy on top to press them down. When the butter has set, the shrimp are ready to eat.

John Lewis

CRABMEAT PIE

No higher compliment can be given the famed Chesapeake Bay blue crab than to serve it in a delicate pie. With herb bread and a fresh fruit salad, a complete luncheon is at hand. For convenience, the pie can be prepared early and refrigerated, then baked later the same morning.

1 pie shell	½ teaspoon salt
2 cups crabmeat	¼ teaspoon mustard
2 teaspoons lemon juice	¼ teaspoon pepper
3 eggs, slightly beaten	1 tablespoon chives or spring
¾ cup sour cream	onion, chopped
½ cup half-and-half	½ cup shredded Swiss cheese

Prebake the pie shell for 3 minutes. Place the crabmeat in the pie shell. Mix the rest of the ingredients, except for the cheese, and pour over the crabmeat. Top with shredded cheese and bake at 375 degrees for 40 minutes.

G.D. Dunlap

FAVORITE BROILED FISH

You will note that this recipe includes no salt, sugar, or fat. These ingredients may be added or substituted according to taste. For example, you can use garlic salt for fresh garlic, and so on.

Serves 4

1–1½ pounds fish steaks or fillets	½ teaspoon chili powder
2–3 garlic cloves, minced	3 tablespoons lemon juice
1 teaspoon, in all, black pepper,	¾ cup plain yogurt
cinnamon, and cloves	

Place the fish in a broiler pan. Combine the remaining ingredients and spread the mixture over the fish. Marinate 1 hour. Broil 5–8 minutes, turning and basting with the sauce until the fish flakes easily. This may be done over a charcoal or other grill.

Jane Brooks

CLAM FRITTERS

When my father-in-law would put on a clambake, he would always deep-fry some clam fritters ahead of time so people wouldn't give up and go home during that long interval during which the bake never seems to get quite done. So I have always eaten these fritters as sort of an hors d'oeuvre. I never knew a time when they didn't achieve their purpose; no one ever gave up on one of Grampa's bakes, no matter how long it took to get done.

3 quarts quahogs in the shell	1½ cups flour
2 large eggs	2 teaspoons baking powder
⅓ cup milk	salt and pepper

Drain the liquor off the clams (reserve it for making chowder) and grind or finely chop them. You will have about 1 pint. In a mixing bowl, beat the eggs until light and add the milk. Sift the flour with the baking powder and add to the egg mixture. Then add the clams and season highly with salt and pepper. Cook spoonfuls of the mixture in deep fat until golden brown. Have the grease hot enough to make a rolling boil when each fritter is dropped in. If the grease is not hot enough, the fritters will be soggy.

Roger C. Taylor

SPICY FRIED SOLE FILLETS

Serves 4–6

1 small onion, sliced paper thin
4 teaspoons salt
4 fillets of sole or another firm
   whitefish, skinned
½ cup chick-pea flour
¼ cup rice flour
½ teaspoon ground cumin
½ teaspoon cayenne pepper

6 tablespoons cold water
3 cups vegetable oil
1 hot green chili, washed, seeded,
   and finely chopped
1 tablespoon fresh coriander,
   finely chopped
¼ teaspoon *garam masala*

In a small bowl, coat the onion with 3 teaspoons of the salt. Set aside. Rinse the fillets under cold running water and pat them completely dry. Split each fillet once lengthwise, then crosswise into sixths. Sprinkle ½ teaspoon salt over the fish. Set aside. In a deep bowl, make a smooth, thick batter of the chick-pea flour, rice flour, cumin, cayenne pepper, the last ½ teaspoon of salt, and cold water. Coat the fish with the batter. Pour the oil into a 12-inch wok, or pour 2–3 inches of oil into a deep fryer. Heat the oil until it reaches 350 degrees. Fry 4–5 pieces of fish at a time until golden on all sides. Place in a baking dish lined with paper towels and keep warm in an oven at 250 degrees.

    To serve the fish, transfer to a heated platter and sprinkle with chili, coriander, and *garam masala*. Rinse the onion slices, pat them dry, and arrange around the fish.

Nan Kulikauskas

ROAST BUFFALO

The first requirement for this recipe is to catch your buffalo. It will be worth the effort, because I don't know any dish more delicious than the succulent flesh of a whole roasted buffalo. When in our boat *Dancing Girl*, we use much the same method of getting our buffalo as did the American Indians. We spear them at night with the aid of torches. The only improvement is that we use electric lights instead of pine knots. Buffalo can range in size from several pounds to more than 20 pounds. Let's assume yours is about middle size.

---

1 ten-pound buffalo or redfish
(channel bass), blackfish (triple-
tail), rockfish (striped bass), or
any similar fish of baking size
1 box stuffing, such as Stove Top
or similar brand
1 cup small shrimp, peeled
1 stalk celery, very coarsely chopped
2 sweet bay leaves or 4 of the
store-bought kind (bay laurel)

4 cups chicken broth or bouillon
1 tablespoon soy sauce
2 tablespoons Worcestershire sauce
½ teaspoon McCormick's seafood
seasoning (go easy with this stuff)
6 small tomatoes, quartered
2 onions, coarsely chopped
2 lemons or limes, sliced
paprika

Scale and draw the buffalo. Rinse the body cavity carefully to remove any grit. Buffalo are vegetarian bottom-feeding fish. (Yes, I said fish. What did you think I was talking about?) Mix the shrimp into the stuffing, then stuff the fish and skewer the body cavity closed. Cover the bottom of a baking pan with the celery. Place the bay leaves so that they will be distributed under the fish. Set the buffalo in the pan and pour in the broth. Sprinkle the buffalo with soy and Worcestershire sauce, then the McCormick's seasoning. Now surround the buffalo with the tomatoes and onions. Arrange the lemon or lime slices along the top of the fish. Sprinkle liberally with paprika. Cover and bake at 350 degrees for 30 minutes. Uncover and bake 15 minutes more. Test with a fork for doneness. (If you do not have an oven, cover and cook on top of the stove, and when done, brown with a butane torch.)

Warren Norville

SHELLFISH QUICHE

Macho men don't eat quiche—Bah! All the more for me. A tossed salad, this wonderful pie, a glass of white wine, and thou. Who could ask for more?

Serves 4–6

2 tablespoons minced onions
3 tablespoons butter
1 cup cooked, fresh, or canned
   crab, shrimp, or lobster
2 tablespoons white vermouth
¼ teaspoon salt
a pinch of pepper
3 eggs

1 cup whipping cream
1 tablespoon tomato paste
¼ teaspoon salt
a pinch of pepper
1 eight-inch pastry shell,
   partially cooked
¼ cup grated Swiss cheese

Sauté onions in butter until tender, but not brown. Add the seafood and cook for 2 minutes. Add the wine and seasonings. Boil for 1 minute, then allow to cool slightly. Beat the eggs with the cream, tomato paste, and seasonings. Blend in the shellfish and onions. Pour the mixture into the pastry shell and sprinkle the cheese over the top. Bake at 375 degrees in the upper third of the oven for 25–30 minutes until the quiche has puffed and browned.

Harold H. Payson

SCALLOPS TAYLOR ALLEN

Our good friend Taylor Allen runs a marina in Rockport, Maine. His winter hobby is diving for scallops in the icy waters of Penobscot Bay. One blustery afternoon he brought us a share of his morning's harvest and a recipe to go with it. It's become our favorite scallop recipe.

Serves 4

butter for the baking dish
1 pound sea scallops (the big ones), halved if tremendous
half a small bag of Pepperidge Farm herb-seasoned bread crumbs, pounded or
    rolled to get rid of all the big lumps
1 cup mild Cheddar cheese, coarsely shredded
½ pint heavy cream

Thoroughly butter, bottom *and* sides, a deep baking dish large enough to fit all the scallops in one layer. Place the scallops in the dish and sprinkle the bread crumbs over top. Use just enough to cover since too many will overpower the delicate flavor of the scallops. What you do next depends on your taste: Either *sprinkle* the cheese and *drizzle* the cream over top for a crispy casserole, or *smother* the scallops with cheese and cream for a moist and bubbly dish. (We're smotherers.) Bake at 400 degrees for 10 minutes. Serve hot right from the baking dish.

Kathleen Pieri

KULEBIAKA

(SALMON LOAF IN FLAKY CRUST)

This recipe, of Russian origin, is delicious and can be a real showpiece, depending on how much time you want to put into the decoration. It was a big hit at my parents' twenty-fifth anniversary dinner, but the thing itself was so big that there were plenty of leftovers. A cold slice of the loaf with a salad makes a tasty summer lunch.

Serves 8–10

Pastry:
4 cups flour
2 sticks chilled butter, in bits
6 tablespoons chilled shortening
1 teaspoon salt
10–12 tablespoons ice water

Salmon Filling:
3 quarts water
2 cups dry white wine
1 cup onions, coarsely chopped
½ cup celery, coarsely chopped
1 cup carrots, coarsely chopped
10 peppercorns
4½ teaspoons salt
2½-pound piece of fresh salmon
1 stick butter
½ pound mushrooms, thinly sliced

3 tablespoons lemon juice
a dash of pepper
3 cups onions, finely chopped
¼ teaspoon pepper
½ cup unconverted long-grain
 white rice
1 cup chicken stock
⅓ cup minced dill
3 hard-boiled eggs, finely chopped

Additional Ingredients:
butter for the pan
1 egg yolk
1 tablespoon or more cream
1 tablespoon melted butter
1 cup melted butter or 1 cup sour cream

For the pastry, combine the flour, butter, shortening, and salt in a chilled bowl. Blend until like coarse meal. Add 10 tablespoons water, toss lightly, and gather into a ball. If the dough is too crumbly, add, by drops, up to 2 tablespoons more water. Divide in half, wrap each half in wax paper, and refrigerate until firm, about 3 hours.

For the filling, combine in a large pot the water, wine, onion, celery, carrots, peppercorns, and 3 teaspoons salt. Bring to a boil then gently place the salmon in the pot. Simmer 10 minutes or until firm. Remove and flake the fish. In a heavy skillet melt 2 tablespoons butter. Add mushrooms and cook until soft. Remove and toss with lemon juice, ½ teaspoon salt, and a dash of pepper. Melt 4 tablespoons butter and add the finely chopped onions, reserving 1 tablespoonful. Sauté until soft. Stir in 1 teaspoon salt, ¼ teaspoon pepper, then add to the mushrooms. Melt the last 2 tablespoons butter and sauté the reserved onion until soft. Add the rice and cook, stirring, for 3 minutes. Add the stock, bring to a boil, and cover tightly. Simmer about 10 minutes or until the rice has absorbed the liquid. Remove pan from heat and mix in the dill, then add rice to the cooked mushrooms and onions, mixing in the chopped egg and salmon. Taste for seasoning.

To assemble the loaf, roll one ball of dough into a rectangle about 1 inch thick. Dust with flour and roll until ⅛ inch thick. Trim to a 7 x 16-inch rectangle. Transfer to a large, heavily buttered cookie sheet. Mound the filling on the dough, leaving a 1-inch border all around. Mix the egg yolk and cream then brush the border with some of the mixture. Roll the other ball of dough into a 9 x 18-inch rectangle and place over top. Trim to even off edges. Seal the edges by rolling them together toward the center then pressing down hard with a fork, your fingers, or a pastry crimper. Cut a 1-inch circle from the center of the top crust. Use this and other trimmings to make decorative shapes such as leaves, cables, or scrolls. Have fun! It will look beautiful. Before decorating, however, coat the entire surface with the remaining egg yolk and cream, then decorate, brush again, and refrigerate 20 minutes. Pour the tablespoon of melted butter into the open circle. Bake at 400 degrees for 1 hour or until golden brown. Garnish with whatever strikes your fancy—dill or parsley sprigs, lemon rounds, cherry tomatoes, or strips of sweet red pepper. Accompany with a pitcher of melted butter or sour cream.

Lori Renn

KING CRAB QUICHE

Serves 8

The Quiche:
1 unbaked pastry shell
2 pounds crabmeat
1 stick butter
a sprinkle of light rum
8 eggs

4 cups light cream
½ teaspoon salt
¼ teaspoon pepper
paprika

The Sauce:
2 sticks butter
¼ cup light rum
1 tablespoon chopped parsley

Line a 9 x 13-inch pan with pastry. Sauté the crab in butter. Sprinkle with light rum. Beat the eggs and cream, and add the salt and pepper. Distribute the crab evenly over the pastry-lined pan, cover it with the egg mixture, and sprinkle with paprika. Bake at 450 degrees for 10 minutes, reduce heat to 350 degrees, and continue baking until the custard sets, about 30 minutes. Remove the quiche from the oven and let it set 10–15 minutes before removing from the pan. For the sauce, melt the butter, then add the light rum and parsley. Serve the quiche hot, with the rum butter poured over the top.

June Ellam

Zarzuela

Serves 4

1 onion, chopped	1 dozen mussels in the shell
2 garlic cloves, minced	1–2 pounds lobster meat, scallops,
3 tablespoons cooking oil	shrimp, or a combination
2 green peppers, chopped	salt and black pepper to taste
1 large can tomatoes in tomato	1 tablespoon dried, crushed red
purée	pepper
1 dozen clams in the shell	boiled rice

In a large skillet or pot sauté the onion and garlic in cooking oil. When the onion is clear and soft, add the green pepper. Add the tomatoes and stir. Next add the mussels, clams, and other seafood. Season with salt, black pepper, and red pepper. Cook for about 20 minutes or until clams and mussels have opened. Serve over rice.

Michael Martin Cohen, M.D.

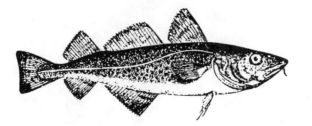

CREAMED CODFISH

Serve this dish with mashed potatoes and a green vegetable such as broccoli or spinach. For variation, add curry powder to the sauce and serve with rice.

---

1 package or wooden box of salt cod	½ cup flour
cold water to cover	2–2½ cups milk
4 tablespoons butter or margarine	salt, if needed, and pepper

---

Cover the codfish with cold water and soak it overnight or for several hours, changing the water 3–4 times. Boil the fish gently, continuing to change the water until you are sure, by tasting the fish, that it is tender and all the salt is out. Place the fish on a plate and cut away any hard crust, then separate the flakes. Melt the butter in the top of a double boiler. Stir in the flour. Add the milk a little at a time until you have a smooth, saltless cream sauce. Add the codfish flakes and keep the mixture hot over boiling water until the sauce absorbs the flavor of the fish. Add salt, only if needed, at the last. Add pepper and serve.

Mrs. Weston Farmer

SOLE WITH DILL AND GINGER STUFFING

Serves 4

4 eight-ounce fillets of sole, flounder, or another firm whitefish, skinned	7 tablespoons clarified butter
	1 garlic clove, slightly crushed
2 tablespoons lemon juice, freshly squeezed	1 tablespoon fresh ginger root, scraped and finely chopped
2 teaspoons salt	¼ cup onions, finely chopped
½ teaspoon black pepper, freshly ground	¼ teaspoon cayenne pepper
	¼ teaspoon turmeric
	¾ cup fresh dill, finely minced

Rinse the fillets under cold running water and pat them dry. Sprinkle both sides with the lemon juice, 1 teaspoon of salt, and black pepper. Marinate at room temperature for 10–15 minutes. Heat 4 tablespoons clarified butter in a skillet over moderate heat until a drop of water sizzles as soon as it hits the fat. Stirring after each addition, add the garlic, ginger, onion, cayenne pepper, turmeric, dill, and remaining teaspoon of salt. Stirring constantly, sauté over low heat until the onions are soft and golden brown. Remove the skillet from the heat and adjust the seasoning. Divide the filling among the fillets, spreading it evenly over each. Starting at the narrow end, roll the fillets and secure them with 2–3 toothpicks.

In a flameproof casserole dish just large enough to hold the rolled fish, heat the remaining 3 tablespoons butter over moderate heat. With the tongue of the roll facing down, cook uncovered for 5 minutes. Transfer the dish to the middle shelf of the oven and bake at 350 degrees for 12 minutes or until the rolls are firm to the touch. Then broil for a few minutes to lightly brown the fish. Bring the liquid that cooked out of the fish to a rapid boil and stir until well blended. Pour the sauce over the fish and serve.

Nan Kulikauskas

SHRIMP CREOLE

1 stick butter
2 tablespoons minced onion
2 tablespoons minced green pepper
2 tablespoons diced celery
½ cup flour

1 teaspoon salt
½ teaspoon paprika
3 cups milk
4 cups cooked shrimp
boiled rice

In the butter sauté the onion, green pepper, and celery. Add the flour, salt, paprika, and milk. Cook until creamy, then add the shrimp. Serve over rice or toast.

April Jenkins

CURRIED SHRIMP

Serves 3–4

4 tablespoons flour
4 tablespoons butter
2 cups milk
¼ teaspoon pepper
½ teaspoon salt
a pinch of ginger adds bite

1 teaspoon curry powder, or more
  to taste
1½ teaspoons lemon juice
  (or 2 teaspoons sherry)
2 cups cooked shrimp
boiled rice

To make the white sauce, heat the flour and butter in a saucepan until the mixture bubbles. Cook, stirring, for 1 minute. Remove from the heat and add the milk. Stir over the fire until thickened, adding the seasonings and, if the sauce is too thick, more milk. Before serving, blend the lemon juice or sherry into the sauce. Stir in the shrimp. Serve over rice.

Howard Barnes

CRABMEAT AND SPINACH NOODLES

This casserole can be baked in the oven, but it can be made just as easily on top of the stove, if you are to go through life with a two-burner stove, as we do in our boat *Dancing Girl*. The oven method is my wife, Harriet's, favorite recipe, and it is, as they say in Louisiana, "some good!" (If you cannot get crabmeat, substitute chicken. One time I even used chipped beef, and it turned out quite well.)

Serves 6–8

1 package spinach noodles	8 ounces sour cream
water to cover	a dash of pepper sauce
2 eggs, separated if you have time	1 pound white crabmeat
1 can Cheddar cheese soup	grease for the baking dish
1 can mushroom soup	grated cheese

Boil the noodles in lightly salted water according to package directions. Drain well. Separate the eggs and beat the whites. Combine the yolks, soups, sour cream, pepper sauce, and crabmeat. Fold in the beaten egg whites. Layer the noodles and the crab mixture in a greased casserole dish. Top with grated cheese. Bake at 350 degrees for 25–30 minutes or until bubbly.

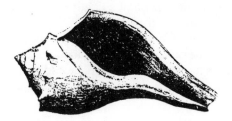

Warren Norville

ESCALLOPED OYSTERS AND CORN

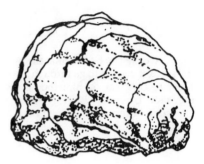

Ah, the Chincoteague Oyster! If you are not one of the brave souls who enjoys them on the half shell, we hope you will join our many friends and family who consider this one of their favorite ways to include oysters in holiday meals and buffet suppers during the "R" months (the ones that end in "R").

Serves 8

1 quart oysters	salt and pepper
2 cups saltines, rolled into crunchy bits	1 stick melted butter
	⅓ cup milk or cream
oil for the baking dish	paprika
2 cups frozen yellow corn, thawed	parsley

Drain the oysters and save the liquid. Remove all pieces of shell. Put a layer of cracker crumbs in the bottom of a lightly oiled 2-quart casserole dish. Add a layer of corn, season with salt and pepper, then add a layer of oysters. Repeat. Top with crumbs and butter. Combine the oyster juice with the milk and pour over the casserole until it is about half an inch from the top. Bake at 450 degrees for 30 minutes or until heated through, but not so as to overcook the delicate oysters! Garnish with paprika and fresh parsley.

G.D. Dunlap

WILD BROOK TROUT

Recipes don't apply here. More to the point is a respect for wild flesh (ask a cat). Speckled trout have much in common with vegetables: The fresher the better. And, like love letters, not to be burned. If a fish is brilliant in the water, it will eat brilliantly. Pink flesh, the native version, is far more palatable than the state-stocked, gray-fleshed variety.

---

speckled trout	pepper
much sweet butter	fresh Italian parsley
a touch of bacon fat	fresh lemon juice

In a medium-hot, thick iron skillet melt the butter and bacon fat until the butter just turns brown. Pepper then cook the fish—about 3 minutes each side for a 14-inch fish—but this you learn from practice. Serve with snips of parsley and lemon juice (no squeeze bottles).

Craig Gilborn

POULET RICKENBACKER

On the occasion when I sampled this dish, I was alone on a singlehanded race across the Tasman Sea in which I did not seem to be doing too well, as taking to the life raft dropped my speed to a shade over one knot, even under favorable conditions. I have named this dish after another gourmet who also enjoyed this highly specialized collation. A word of advice: This dish is practically inedible if not dressed with the correct sauce.

Prepare the sauce by abstinence from food for 10–14 days. Catch and skin a seagull. The skin is too tough to eat, but makes good fish bait. The feathers are a nuisance in a life raft. The disjointed seagull may be consumed either warm or cold, although the former is usually preferred. Whether the entrails are incorporated into the dish depends on the exact quantity of sauce available.

Bill Belcher

CRISPY-CRUNCHY BAKED FISH

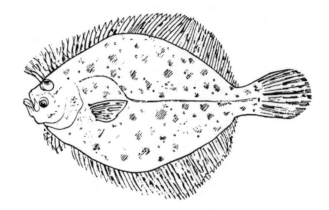

Serves 4

1½–2 pounds trout, sole, or
  flounder
¼ cup whole-wheat flour
¼ cup Grape Nuts cereal
½ teaspoon garlic powder

½ teaspoon onion powder
1 tablespoon chopped fresh parsley
½ cup plain low-fat or nonfat
  yogurt
lemon slices or wedges

Rinse the fish under running water and remove the scales. Mix the dry
ingredients and the parsley. Dip the fish in the yogurt, then in the flour
mixture. Place the fish in a shallow, heated, foil-lined baking dish. Bake at
400 degrees for 20–25 minutes. For a crisper crust, broil an extra 2–3
minutes. Garnish with lemon.

Jane Brooks

SEAFOOD ON A SKEWER

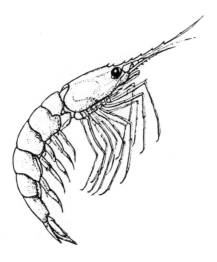

Serves 6

12 ounces shelled shrimp
12 ounces cod or other fish fillets,
  cut into large pieces
6 green peppers, cut into large
  squares

6 onions, cut into large squares
24 cherry tomatoes
1 tablespoon lemon juice
½ cup dry white wine

Using 12 skewers, alternate shrimp and fish with vegetables, beginning and ending with tomatoes. Blend the lemon juice and wine and brush over each skewer. Bake at 350 degrees until the fish is opaque, then place under the broiler for 1–2 minutes.

Pat Feener

RUSSELL PIPI FRITTERS

Living in the Bay of Islands, New Zealand, has many advantages. The beaches near the township of Russell are the home of a variety of shellfish, among them cockles and pipis, similar to clams. They are gathered at low tide where the sand meets the mud and are left soaking in a bucket of sea water for a couple of hours so that they spit out the sand. Pipis should be rinsed well in sweet water before cooking.

Serves 4

The Batter:
1 cup flour
1 egg
1 heaping teaspoon baking powder
1 teaspoon curry powder
milk as needed

The Main Ingredients:
2 cups raw shellfish, washed and
   finely minced
1 cup finely chopped onion
1 tomato, diced
chopped parsley
salt and pepper
cooking oil

Mix the batter ingredients until thick. Add the shellfish, onion, tomato, and parsley. Mix and season with salt and pepper. Heat the cooking oil in a skillet and, when hot, spoon in batter to make 4-inch fritters. When the surface is bubbly, turn them over. Eat the fritters hot—good with yogurt and a big salad.

Eva Palasti Brown

Hot Peppered Crab

For scorching summer days, this family favorite from the Chesapeake is a winner. It is quick, will keep well if refrigerated, and travels well in a cooler. The best way to end a day's sail is with a picnic on the beach or in a park—just this dish and a salad.

Serves 6

water to suit a pot with a
   steaming rack
1 tablespoon ginger
1½ teaspoons celery salt
1½ teaspoons black pepper
1½ teaspoons cayenne pepper
1½ teaspoons cardamom

1½ teaspoons paprika
¾ teaspoon dry mustard
6 crushed cloves
2 bay leaves
3 dozen blue crabs in their
   shells, well rinsed

Fill the pot with water to just below the steaming rack. Bring to a boil. Meanwhile, mix the spices in a small bowl. Place a layer of crabs on the rack and sprinkle liberally with the spice mixture. Repeat this process until all the crabs are layered and coated. Cover the pot and steam the crabs for 20 minutes. Let cool, then chill well. Serve with beer on a well-protected table (newspapers make appropriate tablecloths). Those who like less spicy foods can rinse the spices off the shells before opening the crabs.

Paul Lipke

STUFFED MACKEREL

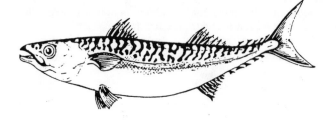

6 mackerel
1 large cooking apple
the juice and rind of 1 lemon
a little water
6 ounces bread crumbs

salt and pepper
a pinch of tarragon, mixed herbs,
    or chopped parsley
1 egg, beaten

Clean and bone the fish. Peel and core the apple and chop. Cook the apple with the lemon juice, rind, and water until soft. When cool, mix with bread crumbs, salt, pepper, and herbs. Bind with beaten egg. Fill the mackerel with this mixture and wrap individually in foil. Bake in a moderate oven (350 degrees) for about 25 minutes.

Chris Thompson

JUDITH'S OLD BAKED HALIBUT

Judith found an old slab of halibut in the bottom of her freezer. God only knows how long it had been there. The length of time wasn't something she wanted to dwell upon. As one might expect, it had dried a bit during storage. Judith was interested in masking some of the freezer flavor and in restoring a bit of life and moistness to the flesh. She was also interested in investing minimum labor in the process. Here's how it went.

1 old slab of frozen halibut, about 1½ inches thick and 10 inches square	a touch of salt and pepper
	Tillamook cheese, in strips
	Parmesan cheese, grated
½ cup milk	a bit of lemon juice
dots of butter	broccoli, cut in long, thin strips

She thawed the old fish and into a large, flat glass baking pan it went. It just fit perfectly. On top went some milk, butter, salt, pepper, some substantial strips of Tillamook cheese (a mild Cheddar, like Longhorn), a liberal sprinkling of Parmesan, and the lemon juice. I could get more exact on amounts, but this kind of fast-and-loose cooking is more intuitive than precise. Over the top of it all went the broccoli, closely packed, with the heads at alternating ends. (Judith is a Virgo, so the spacing of the broccoli was exact.) Then she covered the whole thing with a layer of aluminum foil. Into the oven it went and she baked it at about 350 degrees for about half an hour, testing from time to time with a fork until the flesh flaked apart properly. The old baked halibut was eaten in a mildly warm state, and it was pretty fine stuff.

Mark White

Marinated Fish

This dish is from the kitchen of Brigette Sass, who sailed to Russell, New Zealand, from Hamburg, Germany, on the yacht *Brisa I*. Her husband, Heino Sass, is now a fisherman in the Bay of Islands, and Brigette makes good use of the fresh whitefish fillets he brings home.

Serves 6

2–2½ pounds any whitefish fillets
3 tablespoons whole-meal flour
10 tablespoons olive oil

The Marinade:

2 cups cider vinegar
½ cup water
4 onions, sliced in thin rings
garlic
2 bay leaves
1 dried red chili pepper
2 tablespoons sugar

2 teaspoons salt
black pepper, freshly ground
If available:
   a dash of pickling spices
   a few juniper berries
   dill seed or mustard seeds

The Garnish:

sprigs of dill or parsley

Cut the fillets into small pieces. Wash and dry them, then roll them in the flour. Fry in the hot oil for 5 minutes, until golden brown on all sides. Put on absorbent paper to drain the oil off.

    To prepare the marinade, in a pan boil all marinade ingredients except salt and pepper, and save a few onion rings for the garnish. After 5 minutes boiling add salt and pepper. Place the fish pieces in a wide, flat bowl and completely cover them with hot marinade. Place a few onion rings and sprigs of dill or parsley on top, cover with aluminum foil, and keep in the refrigerator for 2 days before serving. It will keep for 2 weeks.

Eva Palasti Brown

CURRIED COCONUT CLAMS

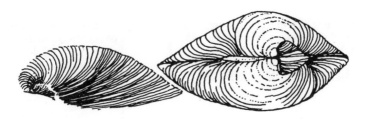

Serves 6

¼ cup vegetable oil
1 tablespoon fresh ginger root,
  scraped and finely chopped
2 large onions, thinly sliced
1 teaspoon salt
2 tablespoons ground coriander
1½ teaspoons turmeric
4 dozen small hard-shell clams,
  washed and thoroughly scrubbed

1 fresh coconut, shelled, peeled,
  and coarsely grated
1 tablespoon lemon juice,
  freshly squeezed
1 tablespoon fresh coriander,
  finely chopped
½ teaspoon cayenne pepper

Use a heavy skillet that has a tightly fitting cover. In the skillet, heat the oil over moderate heat. Stir in the ginger, then the onions. Stirring constantly, sauté the onions until soft and golden brown. Stir in the salt and ground coriander, cook for a minute, then add the turmeric. Cook another minute or so. Add the clams, coating them evenly with the seasoned oil. Cover tightly, reduce the heat to low, and steam 10 minutes, or until the clams open. Transfer the contents of the skillet onto a heated dish. Sprinkle the coconut, then the lemon juice, fresh coriander, and cayenne pepper over the clams. Serve at once.

Nan Kulikauskas

SUZANNE'S BARBECUED SHARK

An excellent fish entrée is thresher (or your favorite) shark steak with an Italian flavor, plus a smoky barbecue taste. The steaks may be cut into serving-size pieces to fit the junior grills found on many boats. If a hamburger-turning grill is available, the essential coating of Italian dressing may be kept intact. I can guarantee that this dish will dispel for all time the age-old repugnance some people have for eating shark.

thresher shark steaks or cutlets, 1 inch thick
Bernstein's Italian dressing (no other seasoning required)

Marinate each cutlet in the dressing for 1 hour or longer. Brush both sides with more dressing and, when the coals are hot, place the steaks on the grill. Cook 5 minutes per side or until flesh shows flakiness. Cover with a foil tent for the smoky accent.

Fred P. Bingham

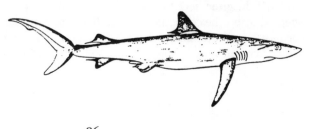

BAKED DORADO

Our dream cruise was almost over. Having spent the summer of 1977 in Scandinavia and the fall off the coasts of Europe and Africa, we were whiling away the winter cruising the West Indies. Late one day in March, while romping through the Bahamas on the northeast trades, our trolling line picked up a dorado between Great Inagua and Mira Por Vos Passage. The next day, anchored in the lee of Crooked Island, Martha served it as the pièce de résistance of an elegant meal, a celebration of an even keel and a quiet boat. Initiated with rum punch and capped with demitasse and Grand Marnier, the meal was accompanied by an Alsatian gewürztraminer. The next time I would try a German Riesling.

1 fresh dorado	fresh parsley, chopped
grease for the pan	½ cup slivered almonds
melted butter	½ stick butter
lemon juice, freshly squeezed	lemon wedges

Place the fish in a greased baking pan and coat it with melted butter. Squeeze the lemon juice over it and sprinkle with parsley. Bake at 350 degrees for about 25 minutes, until done. Sauté the almonds in the butter and sprinkle them over the fish. Serve with lemon wedges.

Brainerd Chapman

GLADYS TWIGG'S IMPERIAL CRAB

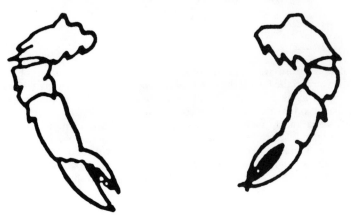

Gladys Twigg, a friend of the Hendersons, is locally noted for her preparation of Chesapeake seafood.

Serves 4

1 pound backfin crabmeat
2 tablespoons minced onion
1 tablespoon minced green pepper
1 tablespoon minced parsley
3 tablespoons melted butter
1 teaspoon salt
⅛ teaspoon pepper

1 teaspoon dry mustard
1 teaspoon Worcestershire sauce
a dash of Tabasco sauce
2 tablespoons mayonnaise
2 egg yolks, slightly beaten
greased scallop shells
½ teaspoon mayonnaise per shell

Pick through the crabmeat to remove any shell or membrane. Simmer the minced onion, green pepper, and parsley in the butter. Mix the seasonings, mayonnaise, and egg yolks and combine with the sautéed vegetables. Gently add the crabmeat to this mixture so you don't break up the crabmeat lumps. Mound the crab mixture high in the greased shells. Top with mayonnaise. Bake at 425 degrees for 20 minutes.

Richard Henderson

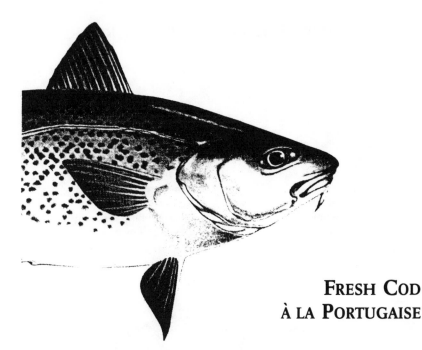

FRESH COD
À LA PORTUGAISE

Serves 4

4 thick, fresh cod fillets	a sprig of thyme
pepper	3 tomatoes, peeled, seeded, and
1 onion, finely chopped	coarsely chopped
1 garlic clove, crushed	½ cup dry white wine
¼ cup parsley, coarsely chopped	1 tablespoon butter

Season fillets with pepper and place in a heavy saucepan. Add the onion, garlic, parsley, thyme, tomatoes, and wine. Bring to a boil, reduce the heat, and simmer gently, covered, for about 10 minutes. Remove the fish carefully, arrange it on a hot serving dish, and keep warm. Reduce the cooking liquid by a third, correct the seasoning, and finish by adding the butter: Allow it to melt without stirring. Pour the sauce over the fish and serve at once.

Jonathan Eaton

WEST INDIAN FISH PUDDING

1 pound raw snapper, grouper,
    or another whitefish
1 stick butter, softened
1 teaspoon salt
pepper, freshly ground
3 eggs, slightly beaten
4 tablespoons flour

1⅔ cups milk
⅔ cup cream
grease for the pan
buttered bread crumbs
parsley, sliced cucumbers, and
    cooked shrimp for garnish
Hollandaise sauce

Remove skin and bones from fish. Grind fish and place in a bowl. Add butter, salt, and pepper. Mix thoroughly, adding, alternately, the egg and flour. Gradually add milk and cream, beating well. If the mixture curdles, place the bowl in simmering water and beat until smooth. Grease a loaf pan and coat the inside with the bread crumbs. Fill the loaf pan three-quarters full, put the pan in a dish of boiling water, cover the pudding with waxed paper, and bake in a slow oven for 1½ hours. Test for doneness with a thin blade. Garnish with parsley, sliced cucumbers, and shrimp. Serve with Hollandaise sauce.

Ross Norgrove

MACKEREL IN OATMEAL

One evening on a passage for the Western Isles, we put a line with spinners over the side and within a few minutes had six beautiful mackerel. It was dark as we came into Buckie on the Moray Firth, and the mackerel were already in the pan. Eaten within an hour of being caught, they were a dish fit for a king.

---

6 fresh mackerel
oatmeal
salt and pepper

1 tablespoon butter
lemon juice, freshly squeezed

After having cleaned the fish well, open them out flat and dry them with kitchen paper. Then roll them in a mixture of oatmeal, salt, and pepper. Melt the butter in a frying pan. When it begins to sizzle, put the fish in, skin side up. Cook for a few minutes, then turn over carefully. Finish the cooking rather more slowly with the pan covered. Ten minutes in all should be enough. Just before serving, squeeze lemon juice over the fish.

John Lewis

SIMPLE SALMON CASSEROLE

Serves 6

1 cup dry bread crumbs
1 cup scalded milk
1 can red salmon, boned and flaked
2 well-beaten eggs
2 tablespoons melted butter

1 tablespoon lemon juice
2 tablespoons chopped onion
salt and pepper
oil for the baking dish

Soak bread crumbs in milk, then combine with salmon, eggs, butter, lemon juice, and onion. Mix lightly and season with salt and pepper. Pour into an oiled baking dish. Bake at 425 degrees for about 20 minutes.

Ardie Millay

FETTUCINE WITH CRAB AND ZUCCHINI

Serves 2–3

½ pound zucchini, thinly sliced
2 tablespoons butter
3 mushrooms, thinly sliced
1 green onion, chopped
6–8 ounces crabmeat, cooked and
   flaked
½ cup chicken stock

2 teaspoons lemon juice,
   freshly squeezed
salt, pepper, and oregano
2 tablespoons heavy cream
¼ cup grated Parmesan cheese
¼ pound fettucine
cherry tomatoes
parsley sprigs

In a large skillet sauté zucchini in butter until just tender. Stir in mushrooms and onion. Add crabmeat, stock, lemon juice, salt, pepper, and oregano. Simmer 1 minute, then stir in the cream and 2 tablespoons of the Parmesan. Keep warm. Cook fettucine in boiling, oiled, salted water for 10–12 minutes or until *al dente*. Drain and turn onto a heated serving dish. Spoon the sauce over the pasta and toss lightly. Garnish with remaining cheese, the tomatoes, and the parsley.

Nan Kulikauskas

EASY HERBED FISH

Serves 4

1 pound fresh or frozen fish fillets
grease for the pan
pepper
2 tablespoons mayonnaise or salad
   dressing

1½ teaspoons fresh tarragon leaves,
   finely chopped (or ½ teaspoon
   crushed, dried tarragon)
½ teaspoon Dijon-style mustard
paprika
4 orange wedges

Thaw fish, if frozen. Divide into 4 serving-size pieces and place them on the greased rack of a broiler pan. Sprinkle with freshly ground pepper. In a bowl combine the mayonnaise, tarragon, and mustard. Spread the mixture evenly over the fish. Broil 4 inches from the heat for 5–7 minutes or until the fish flakes easily when tested with a fork. Sprinkle with paprika and serve with orange wedges.

Pat Feener

IMPRESSIVE, BUT EASY, STUFFED SOLE

This dish looks and tastes like something you really worked at, but it's actually quite easy. You can even prepare it in the morning and keep it covered in the refrigerator until you're ready to bake it for the evening meal.

To prove the point: I once prepared this on the day my husband and I were to entertain a man my husband was building a boat for—the man also happened to be the former manager of New York's Plaza Hotel. I was so nervous that I dropped the whole dish on the way from the refrigerator to the oven. There was enough time to send my husband out for more fish, make new stuffing, and have the meal on the table right on schedule. Success!

Serves 4

The Stuffing:
½ cup chopped celery
½ cup chopped onion
3 tablespoons melted butter
½ teaspoon salt
½ teaspoon sage, thyme, or both
2 tablespoons lemon juice
2 cups soft bread crumbs
1 egg, beaten

The Fish:
2 pounds thin sole fillets
salt and pepper
butter for the baking dish

The Sauce:
½ cup melted butter
3 tablespoons lemon juice

The Garnish:
parsley and lemon slices

Start with the stuffing. Sauté the celery and onion in butter for 8 minutes or until tender. Add the salt, herbs, and lemon juice. Mix thoroughly, then add the bread crumbs and egg. Season each fillet with salt and pepper. Place a ball of stuffing on the rounded end of each fillet and roll it up, securing the roll with a toothpick. Place the rolled fillets side by side in a deep, buttered baking dish. Pour a lemon-butter sauce, made by combining the melted butter and lemon juice, over the whole dish. Bake at 450 degrees for 20 minutes. Transfer to a heated platter, garnish, and serve.

Kathleen Pieri

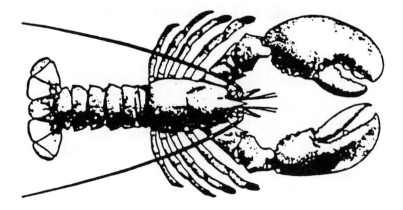

LOBSTER NEWBURG

3 tablespoons margarine
3 tablespoons flour
½ teaspoon salt
1½ cups milk
2 cups cooked, chopped lobster
   pieces

1 cup sliced celery
2 tablespoons chili sauce
2 teaspoons lemon juice
a dash of paprika
boiled rice
parsley or olive slices

Melt the margarine in a saucepan and blend in the flour and salt. Remove the pan from the heat. Gradually add the milk, stirring until the mixture is smooth. Cook the sauce over medium heat, stirring constantly until the mixture comes to a boil. Reduce the heat and simmer the sauce for 1 minute. Add the lobster pieces, celery, chili sauce, lemon juice, and paprika. Heat. Serve the lobster newburg over rice, garnished with sprigs of parsley or olive slices.

Wanda Clossey

CRABMEAT AND CHEESE SOUFFLÉ

This recipe came from Minnesota, as I used to go out there frequently. The Scandinavians are so seafood-minded that seafood in some form was served at every luncheon or cocktail party.

8 ounces crabmeat	1½ cups grated cheese
4 tablespoons melted butter	a pinch of salt
1½ cups milk	2 eggs, separated
2 tablespoons flour	butter for the baking dish

Mix together all ingredients except the egg whites, which should be beaten then folded in. Pour the mixture into a buttered baking dish and set in a pan of hot water. Bake at 350 degrees for 30 minutes.

Eleanor Stephens
(daughter of W.P. Stephens)

ARTHUR TREACHER–STYLE FISH

3 pounds fish fillets
buttermilk to cover
1 lemon, sliced

3 cups cooking oil
3–4 cups dry pancake mix
2½ cups club soda

Soak the fish fillets in just enough dairy buttermilk to cover them. Slice the lemon over the fish and refrigerate in a covered container for 2–3 hours to remove the fishy taste. Heat the oil in a heavy 2½-quart saucepan. Drain the milk from the fish. Cut each fillet in half (makes triangles). Dredge fish in 1–2 cups pancake mix. In a bowl combine the remaining 2 cups of pancake mix with the club soda to give the batter the consistency of buttermilk. Dip the fillets into the batter, letting the excess drip off into the bowl. Deep-fry 4 minutes on each side. Without heaping, keep the fried pieces warm in an oven at 250 degrees until all are done.

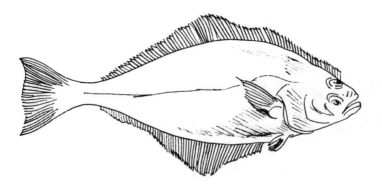

Ardie Millay

CURRIED HALIBUT WITH TOMATOES

Serves 4

4 eight-ounce halibut steaks, sliced
  1 inch thick and cut lengthwise
  in half
2 tablespoons lemon juice,
  freshly squeezed
1½ teaspoons salt
½ teaspoon black pepper,
  freshly ground
¼ cup vegetable oil

½ cup onions, finely chopped
¼ teaspoon cayenne pepper
¼ teaspoon turmeric
2 teaspoons ground coriander
3 tomatoes, coarsely chopped
4 tablespoons fresh coriander,
  finely chopped
1 tablespoon vegetable oil
¼ teaspoon *garam masala*

Rinse the fish under cold running water and pat them dry. Sprinkle both sides with the lemon juice, 1 teaspoon of the salt, and the black pepper. Marinate at room temperature for 10–15 minutes. Heat the oil in a skillet over moderate heat and sauté the onions until they are soft and golden brown. Do not let them burn. Add the remaining ½ teaspoon of salt, the cayenne pepper, turmeric, and ground coriander. Stir well. Add the tomatoes and 2 tablespoons of the fresh coriander and transfer the contents of the skillet into a bowl. Pour the tablespoon of oil into the skillet, then add the fish. Spread the tomato mixture on top of that. Sprinkle with *garam masala*, cover tightly, and cook over low heat for 8–10 minutes or until firm and easily flaked. Serve the fish and its sauce on a heated platter and topped with the rest of the fresh coriander.

Nan Kulikauskas

FISH HASH

Whenever you bring home more fish than you can eat for dinner, try this fish hash for the next day. It was a favorite of Captain Edward A. McFarland of New Harbor, Maine. He attributed it to Old Man Meserve, who was "strong on fish hash." In this recipe, quantities are not important. You can't very well wreck it.

about 3 slices salt pork
1 medium-sized onion, cut up quite small
some potatoes, boiled or baked, then cut up
fish, corned hake for choice, but any fish will do, cooked and cut in chunks

Fry up the salt pork. Start the onion frying as soon as any grease appears. Add the potatoes and fry until brown. Add the fish. Any stuffing or gelatin in the dish does nothing but good. Heat everything up until the ingredients have made each others' acquaintance and the whole panful has a homogeneous appearance.

Roger Duncan

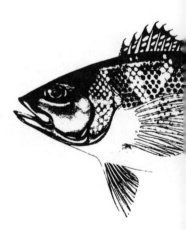

Easy Fish Sticks

2 eggs
1 teaspoon salt
½ teaspoon pepper
1 cup flour
¾ cup milk

1 heaping teaspoon baking powder
a squirt of lemon juice
fish, cut into pieces
vegetable oil for frying

With a mixer, beat together the eggs, salt, pepper, flour, milk, baking powder, and lemon juice. Dip the fish pieces in batter and deep-fry in *hot* fat for 3–6 minutes or until golden brown.

April Jenkins

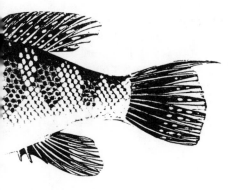

PACKET OF FISH PROVENÇAL

There are endless variations to this recipe: Use any combination of liquids (even orange juice is good with some fish), vegetables or fruit, and seasonings, such as grated cheese. Or make a very thick cream sauce with cheese, mushrooms, or spinach. A quick rummage through the galley lockers or ice chest and you'll find all the ingredients you need to create your own version.

For each serving:

a square of foil, heavy brown paper, or waxed paper
1 fish fillet
lemon juice, vinegar, or white wine
chopped onion, green pepper, tomato, mushrooms
oil or butter
seasonings

Thoroughly oil or butter a foil or paper square large enough to wrap the fillet completely. Place the fish on one side of the square and sprinkle it with juice, vinegar, or wine. Top with chopped vegetables and season as desired. Fold the paper over the fish, tightly crimping the edges to seal the packet. Place it on a cookie sheet or heavy foil and bake at 450 degrees for 10–15 minutes, depending on the thickness of the fillet. If you are using paper, let the paper puff and brown slightly. Place the packet on a dinner plate, slit open, and eat directly from the packet.

Patrick and June Ellam

GREAT SEAFOOD CASSEROLE

¾ pound seafood, any combination
   of cooked lobster or shrimp or
   raw crabmeat, fish, or scallops
3 slices soft bread, cubed
½ cup milk

4 hard-cooked eggs, finely diced
1 teaspoon finely diced onion
1 teaspoon Worcestershire sauce
1 cup mayonnaise
buttered bread crumbs

Combine all ingredients except the buttered bread crumbs and put in a casserole dish. Top with crumbs and bake at 350 degrees for 20 minutes.

April Jenkins

HADDOCK AND TOMATOES

1½ pounds haddock or other firm
  whitefish fillets
2 onions, chopped into small pieces
2 tablespoons butter
salt and pepper

butter for the dish
1 tin Italian tomatoes, drained
2 ounces hard cheese, grated
bread crumbs or flaked millet

Skin the fillets and cut them into 4-inch lengths. Fry the onion in butter until golden and transparent. Put a little onion, salt, and pepper on each piece of fish and roll them up. Butter a casserole dish, put a little onion at the bottom, and arrange the fish and tomatoes alternately in layers. Top with bread crumbs, put the cheese on top, cover, and bake at 350 degrees for 45 minutes. Remove the lid and brown under the broiler to finish the dish.

John Lewis

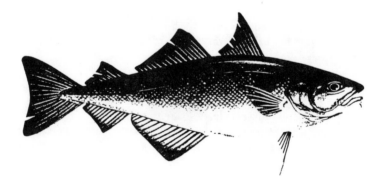

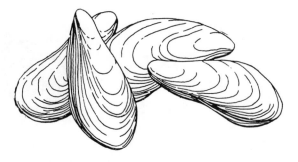

STEAMED MUSSELS

One word of caution: Watch out for pearls. Mussels in some areas secrete tiny pearls, which are of no particular value but cause some embarrassment when chomped on. (And don't sit on the mussel bed to eat your mussels raw.)

---

15 or 20 2–2½-inch blue mussels per serving
water (or half water and half dry white wine) to cover
melted butter

Thoroughly scrub the mussels clean. Place them on a cake rack in a large pot over half an inch of water. Boil the water to steam the mussels for about 15 minutes until they open. Serve hot with a small bowl of melted butter.

Phil Schwind

FISH CASSEROLE WITH ASPARAGUS

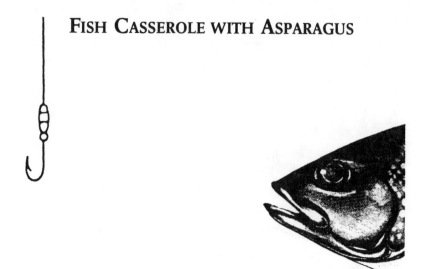

2 pounds whitefish	2 tablespoons flour
dry white wine or cider	milk
a can of asparagus tips	salt and pepper
2 tablespoons butter	grated cheese

Remove the bones and skin from the fish. Poach gently in wine or cider. Drain the fish, reserving the liquor, and place it in a casserole dish with the asparagus. To make the white sauce, melt the butter in a saucepan, then stir in the flour. Add 1 pint of liquid (fish stock and milk) gradually and stir until boiling. Season. Pour the sauce over the fish and asparagus, top with grated cheese, and bake in moderate oven for about 20 minutes.

Chris Thompson

Sole Silvio

Very tasty and quick!

Serves 4

5 tablespoons margarine or butter	½ cup chicken broth
⅛ teaspoon fresh garlic, crushed	½ cup milk
2 tablespoons flour	2 teaspoons lemon juice
¼ teaspoon paprika	1½ pounds sole fillets
a dash of ground white pepper	

Melt 2 tablespoons of margarine in a saucepan over moderate heat. Stir in the garlic and cook for 30 seconds. Stir in the flour, paprika, and pepper. Cook 1 minute. Gradually whisk in the chicken broth, milk, and lemon juice and stir until thickened, about 2 minutes. Keep the sauce warm. Dot the fillets with the remaining 3 tablespoons margarine. Bake or broil until done and serve with the sauce.

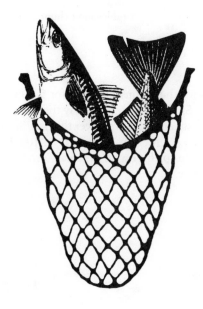

Jonathan Eaton

SPICY BAKED FISH

Chris Thompson operates a small fishing trawler off the Norfolk (England) coast and sends this recipe for any type of leftovers from the catch. It is an ideal way of using up bottom fish.

Serves 4

6 rashers (thin slices) bacon
2 onions, sliced
5 tablespoons butter
½ teaspoon mixed herbs
4 whitefish fillets
salt and pepper

½ pint cheese sauce
2 heaping tablespoons bread crumbs
1 tomato, peeled and sliced
paprika
1 tablespoon chopped parsley

Chop the bacon and sauté with the onions in butter for 5 minutes. Drain and place in a fireproof dish. Sprinkle with herbs, lay the fish on top, and season well. Make the cheese sauce and pour it over the fish. Sprinkle with bread crumbs, and bake at 375 degrees for 30 minutes. After 15 minutes add a border of tomato slices and sprinkle with paprika. Complete cooking, sprinkle with parsley, and serve.

Chris Thompson

Microwave Crab and Spinach Quiche

Serves 6

1 nine-inch pie shell
1 six-ounce package frozen
  crabmeat
4 eggs
1 cup evaporated milk
1 teaspoon prepared mustard

⅛ teaspoon nutmeg
¾ teaspoon salt
2 tablespoons dry sherry
half a ten-ounce package frozen
  chopped spinach, thawed
¾ cup shredded Swiss cheese

Cook the pastry in a glass pie plate. In its original package, thaw the crabmeat on a microwave-proof plate for 3 minutes. In a large bowl, beat the eggs and add the milk, mustard, nutmeg, salt, and sherry. Mix well. Drain the spinach and add with the cheese and crabmeat to the egg mixture. Stir and pour into the pastry shell. Cook on the "bake" setting for 30–35 minutes or until nearly set in the center. Let stand 5 minutes before serving.

Ardie Millay

MACKEREL CHABUKA

This recipe originated many years ago on a safari along the Zambezi River and is wicked with Zambezi bream, one of the most delectable of fish. Here's a recipe for a less exotic species: It is, of course, a variation on trout amandine. Try it with pike, pompano, snapper—almost any fish you like. Delicious when combined with fresh French bread!

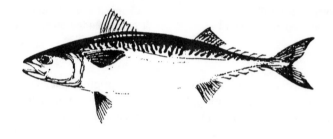

Serves 2

2 fresh, gutted mackerel, straight from the ocean to the pan
salt and pepper
1 egg, lightly beaten
1 cup milk
about 8 tablespoons flour

¼ cup butter, olive oil, or margarine
⅓ cup slivered almonds
¼ cup fresh lemon juice
1 tablespoon Tabasco or Worcestershire sauce
a sprig of parsley, chopped

Clean the mackerel. Salt and pepper to taste. Make a batter of the egg and milk, dip in the fish, then dredge lightly with flour. Heat the butter in a large skillet and fry the mackerel until golden brown, about 5–8 minutes for the average fish. Transfer the cooked mackerel to a serving plate. Add the almonds to the skillet and brown lightly. Then add the lemon juice, Tabasco or Worcestershire sauce, and parsley. Stir and heat through. Pour over the fish to serve.

Brian Fagan

COQUINA

---

10 quarts coquina
2 quarts fresh water

Dig these miniature clams out of any seaside beach, from South Carolina to the Mexican border at Brownsville, Texas. We collect them in a wooden frame with ¼-inch hardware cloth tacked over it. Capsize 'em into a pail and add the fresh water. Let boil over several times. Drain into a pan, let settle, and chill. Serve the coquina hot or cold, and use the broth as a base for fish or conch chowder.

Carl D. Lane

Index